jQuery Mobile Web Development Essentials

Third Edition

Build a powerful and practical jQuery-based framework
in order to create mobile-optimized websites

Raymond Camden

Andy Matthews

[PACKT] open source*

PUBLISHING

community experience distilled

BIRMINGHAM - MUMBAI

jQuery Mobile Web Development Essentials

Third Edition

First published: May 2012

Second edition: September 2013

Third edition: March 2016

Production reference: 1210316

Published by Packt Publishing Ltd.
Livery Place
35 Livery Street
Birmingham B3 2PB, UK.

ISBN 978-1-78355-505-5

www.packtpub.com

Credits

Authors
Raymond Camden
Andy Matthews

Reviewer
Eliecer Daza

Commissioning Editor
Usha Iyer

Acquisition Editor
Kevin Colaco

Content Development Editor
Rashmi Suvarna

Technical Editor
Rahul C. Shah

Copy Editor
Akshata Lobo

Project Coordinator
Judie Jose

Proofreader
Safis Editing

Indexer
Priya Sane

Graphics
Kirk D'Penha

Production Coordinator
Shantanu N. Zagade

Cover Work
Shantanu N. Zagade

About the Authors

Raymond Camden is a developer advocate for IBM. His work focuses on the StrongLoop platform, Bluemix, hybrid mobile development, Node.js, HTML5, and web standards in general. He's a published author and presents at conferences and user groups on a variety of topics. Raymond can be reached at his blog (http://www.raymondcamden.com), @raymondcamden on Twitter, or via e-mail at raymondcamden@gmail.com.

Raymond Camden is the author of many development books, including *Apache Cordova in Action, Manning Publications* and *Client-Side Data Storage, O'Reilly Media, Inc.*

I'd like to thank everyone on the jQuery and jQuery Mobile teams for making tools that have changed my life. Without your hard work and dedication, the Web would be less awesome.

Andy Matthews has been working as a software engineer for nearly 20 years with experience in a wide range of industries and a skillset that includes UI/UX, graphic design, and programming. He is the coauthor of the books *Creating Mobile Apps with jQuery Mobile* and *jQuery Mobile Web Development Essentials* by Packt Publishing. He has written for online publications, such as Adobe, NetTuts, and .NET Magazine. He has spoken at conferences all over the country, and has developed a number of projects for the open source community.

Thanks to Packt for publishing this book. Thanks to the jQuery Mobile team for creating such a great and easy to use open source project.

About the Reviewer

Eliecer Daza has been a web developer since 2005. He has ample experience in Java, Python, Perl, jQuery, and jQuery Mobile being a Java developer for more than 8 years. He has developed software for information management and customer relationship management (CMR) for health promoting enterprises (EPS), public transportation, and education companies in the private and public sectors. He has been working as a Python developer for more than 4 years, working with responsive websites and new languages and technologies.

His main areas of interest lie in the development of Linux, Python, Android, and Google Services. He has a huge interest in nurturing blog spaces about Linux administration and programming.

Look for me on my page at http://www.eliecerdaza.com.

My heartfelt appreciation to God, my beloved mother and friend, my family, and my girlfriend July.

www.PacktPub.com

eBooks, discount offers, and more

Did you know that Packt offers eBook versions of every book published, with PDF and ePub files available? You can upgrade to the eBook version at www.PacktPub.com and as a print book customer, you are entitled to a discount on the eBook copy. Get in touch with us at customercare@packtpub.com for more details.

At www.PacktPub.com, you can also read a collection of free technical articles, sign up for a range of free newsletters and receive exclusive discounts and offers on Packt books and eBooks.

https://www2.packtpub.com/books/subscription/packtlib

Do you need instant solutions to your IT questions? PacktLib is Packt's online digital book library. Here, you can search, access, and read Packt's entire library of books.

Why subscribe?

- Fully searchable across every book published by Packt
- Copy and paste, print, and bookmark content
- On demand and accessible via a web browser

Table of Contents

Preface

What is jQuery Mobile?

On August 11, 2010, nearly six years ago, John Resig (creator of jQuery) announced the jQuery Mobile project. While it focused on the UI framework, it was also a recognition of jQuery itself as a tool for mobile websites and that work would be done to the core framework itself to make it work better on devices. Release after release, the jQuery Mobile project evolved into a powerful framework, encompassing more platforms, more features, and better performance with every update.

But what do we mean when we say a *UI framework*? What does it mean for developers and designers? jQuery Mobile provides a way to turn regular HTML (and CSS) into mobile-friendly websites. As you will see soon in the first chapter, you can take a regular HTML page, add the required bits for jQuery Mobile (essentially, lines of HTML), and your page is transformed into a mobile-friendly version instantly.

Unlike other frameworks, jQuery Mobile is focused on HTML. In fact, for a framework tied to jQuery, you can do a heck of a lot of work without writing one line of JavaScript. It's a powerful, practical way of creating mobile websites that any existing HTML developer can pick up and adapt within a few hours. Compare this to other frameworks, such as Sencha Touch. Sencha Touch is also a powerful framework, but its approach is radically different, using JavaScript to help define and layout pages. jQuery Mobile is much friendlier to people who are more familiar with HTML as opposed to JavaScript. jQuery Mobile is *touch-friendly*, which will make sense to anyone who has used a smartphone and struggled to click the exact spot on a website with tiny text and hard-to-spot links. It will make sense to anyone who has accidentally clicked on a Reset button instead of Submit. jQuery Mobile will enhance your content to help solve these issues. Regular buttons become large, fat, and easy-to-hit buttons. Links can be turned into list-based navigation systems. Content can be split into virtual pages with smooth transitions. You will be surprised just how jQuery Mobile works without writing much code at all.

What's the cost?

Ah, the million dollar question. Luckily, this one is easy to answer: nothing. jQuery Mobile, like jQuery itself, is completely free to use for any purpose. Not only that, it's open source. Don't like how something works? You can change it. Want something not supported by the framework? You can add it. To be fair, digging deep into the code base is probably something most folks will not be comfortable doing. However, the fact that you can if you need to, and the fact that other people can, will lead to a product that will be open to development by the community at large.

What do you need to know?

Finally, along with not paying a dime to get, and work with, jQuery Mobile, the best thing is that you probably already have all the skills necessary to work with the framework. As you will see in the upcoming chapters, jQuery Mobile is an HTML-based framework. If you know HTML, even just simple HTML, you can use the jQuery Mobile framework. Knowledge of CSS and JavaScript is a plus, but not entirely required (while jQuery Mobile uses a lot of CSS and JavaScript behind the scenes, you don't actually have to write any of this yourself!).

What about native apps?

jQuery Mobile does not create native applications. You'll see later in the book how you can combine jQuery Mobile with *hybrid mobile* technologies, such as Apache Cordova, to create native apps; but in general, jQuery Mobile is for building websites. The question on whether to develop a website or a mobile app is not something this book can answer. You need to look at your business needs and see what will satisfy them. Because we are not building mobile apps themselves, you do not have to worry about setting up any accounts with Google or Apple, or paying any fees for the marketplace. Any user with a mobile device that includes a browser will be able to view your mobile-optimized websites.

Again, if you want to develop true mobile apps with jQuery Mobile, it's definitely an option.

Help!

While we'd like to think that this book will cover every single possible topic you would need for all your jQuery Mobile needs, most likely there will be things we can't cover. If you need help, there are a couple of places you can try.

First, the jQuery Mobile docs (`http://jquerymobile.com/demos/`) cover syntax, features, and development in general, much like this book. While the material may cover some of the same ground, if you find something confusing here, try the official docs. Sometimes, a second explanation can really help.

Second, the jQuery Mobile forum (`http://forum.jquery.com/jquery-mobile`) is an open-ended discussion list for jQuery Mobile topics. This is the perfect place to ask questions. Also, it's a good place to learn about problems other people are having. You may even be able to help them. One of the best ways to learn a new topic is by helping others.

What this book covers

Chapter 1, Preparing Your First jQuery Mobile Project, works you through your first jQuery Mobile project. It details what must be added to your project's directory and source code.

Chapter 2, Working with jQuery Mobile Pages, continues the work in the previous chapter and introduces the concept of jQuery Mobile pages.

Chapter 3, Enhancing Pages with Headers, Footers, and Toolbars, explains how to enhance your pages with nicely formatted headers and footers.

Chapter 4, Working with Lists, describes how to create jQuery Mobile list views. These are mobile-optimized lists, which are especially great for navigation.

Chapter 5, Getting Practical – Building a Simple Hotel Mobile Website, walks you through creating your first real (albeit simple) jQuery Mobile application.

Chapter 6, Working with Forms and jQuery Mobile, explains the process of using jQuery Mobile-optimized forms. Layout and special form features are covered in detail.

Chapter 7, Creating Grids, Panels, and Other Widgets, walks you through special jQuery Mobile UI items for creating grid-based layouts and other common UI elements.

Chapter 8, Moving Further with the Notekeeper Mobile Application, walks you through the process of creating another website, an HTML5-enhanced note-taking application.

Chapter 9, jQuery Mobile Configuration, Utilities, and JavaScript Methods, describes the various JavaScript-based utilities your code may have need of.

Chapter 10, Working with Events, details the events thrown by various jQuery Mobile-related features, like pages loading and unloading.

Chapter 11, Enhancing jQuery Mobile, demonstrates how to change the default appearance of your jQuery Mobile websites by selecting and creating unique themes.

Chapter 12, Creating Native Applications, takes what you've learned previously and shows how to use the open source PhoneGap project to create real native applications.

Chapter 13, Becoming an Expert – Building an RSS Reader Application, expands upon the previous chapter by creating an application that lets you add and read RSS feeds on mobile devices.

What you need for this book

Nothing! Technically, you need a computer and a browser as well, but jQuery Mobile is built with HTML, CSS, and JavaScript. No Integrated Development Environment (IDE) or special tool will be required to work with the framework. If you've got any editor on your system (and all operating systems include a free editor of some sort), you can develop with jQuery Mobile.

Who this book is for

This book is for anyone looking to embrace mobile development and expand their skill set beyond the desktop.

Conventions

In this book, you will find a number of text styles that distinguish between different kinds of information. Here are some examples of these styles and an explanation of their meaning.

Code words in text, database table names, folder names, filenames, file extensions, pathnames, dummy URLs, user input, and Twitter handles are shown as follows: "You can find all the source code for this chapter in the c1 folder of the ZIP file you downloaded from GitHub."

A block of code is set as follows:

```
Listing 1-1: test1.html
<html>
  <head>
    <title>First Mobile Example</title>
  </head>
  <body>
```

```
<h1>Welcome</h1>
<p>
Welcome to our first mobile web site. It's going to be the
best site you've ever seen. Once we get some content. And a
business plan. But the hard part is done!
</p>
<p>
<i>Copyright Megacorp &copy; 2015</i>
</p>
</body>
</html>
```

New terms and **important words** are shown in bold. Words that you see on the screen, for example, in menus or dialog boxes, appear in the text like this: "There are a few options here, but you want the **ZIP file** option."

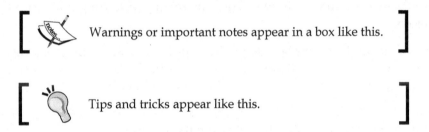

Warnings or important notes appear in a box like this.

Tips and tricks appear like this.

Reader feedback

Feedback from our readers is always welcome. Let us know what you think about this book—what you liked or disliked. Reader feedback is important for us as it helps us develop titles that you will really get the most out of.

To send us general feedback, simply e-mail feedback@packtpub.com, and mention the book's title in the subject of your message.

If there is a topic that you have expertise in and you are interested in either writing or contributing to a book, see our author guide at www.packtpub.com/authors.

Customer support

Now that you are the proud owner of a Packt book, we have a number of things to help you to get the most from your purchase.

Downloading the example code

This book contains many code samples. You are not expected to type them in. You should not type them all in. Rather, you should download them from the public GitHub repository setup for the book: `https://github.com/cfjedimaster/jQuery-Mobile-Book`. The GitHub repository will be updated as typos and other mistakes are found in the book. Therefore, it is possible the code may not match exactly the text in the book.

If you are not familiar with GitHub, then simply click on the **Downloads** tab and then either **Download as zip** or **Download as tar.gz** to quickly get an archived collection of all the files.

You should extract these les onto a local web server. If you do not have one installed, we recommend installing Apache (`http://httpd.apache.org/`). Apache works on all platforms, is free, and is typically easy to install. Once extracted, you can edit these files, view them in your browser, or copy them as a starting point for your own projects.

You can download the example code files for this book from your account at `http://www.packtpub.com`. If you purchased this book elsewhere, you can visit `http://www.packtpub.com/support` and register to have the files e-mailed directly to you.

You can download the code files by following these steps:

1. Log in or register to our website using your e-mail address and password.
2. Hover the mouse pointer on the **SUPPORT** tab at the top.
3. Click on **Code Downloads & Errata**.
4. Enter the name of the book in the **Search** box.
5. Select the book for which you're looking to download the code files.
6. Choose from the drop-down menu where you purchased this book from.
7. Click on **Code Download**.

Once the file is downloaded, please make sure that you unzip or extract the folder using the latest version of:

- WinRAR / 7-Zip for Windows
- Zipeg / iZip / UnRarX for Mac
- 7-Zip / PeaZip for Linux

Downloading the color images of this book

We also provide you with a PDF file that has color images of the
screenshots/diagrams used in this book. The color images will help you
better understand the changes in the output. You can download this file
from `https://www.packtpub.com/sites/default/files/downloads/`
`jQueryMobileWebDevelopmentEssentialsThirdEdition_ColorImages.pdf`.

Errata

Although we have taken every care to ensure the accuracy of our content, mistakes
do happen. If you find a mistake in one of our books—maybe a mistake in the text or
the code—we would be grateful if you could report this to us. By doing so, you can
save other readers from frustration and help us improve subsequent versions of this
book. If you find any errata, please report them by visiting `http://www.packtpub.`
`com/submit-errata`, selecting your book, clicking on the **Errata Submission Form**
link, and entering the details of your errata. Once your errata are verified, your
submission will be accepted and the errata will be uploaded to our website or added
to any list of existing errata under the Errata section of that title.

To view the previously submitted errata, go to `https://www.packtpub.com/books/`
`content/support` and enter the name of the book in the search field. The required
information will appear under the **Errata** section.

Piracy

Piracy of copyrighted material on the Internet is an ongoing problem across all
media. At Packt, we take the protection of our copyright and licenses very seriously.
If you come across any illegal copies of our works in any form on the Internet, please
provide us with the location address or website name immediately so that we can
pursue a remedy.

Please contact us at `copyright@packtpub.com` with a link to the suspected
pirated material.

We appreciate your help in protecting our authors and our ability to bring you
valuable content.

Questions

If you have a problem with any aspect of this book, you can contact us at
`questions@packtpub.com`, and we will do our best to address the problem.

1
Preparing Your First jQuery Mobile Project

You know what jQuery Mobile is, the history of it, as well as its features and goals. Now, we're actually going to build our first jQuery Mobile website (well, web page) and see how easy it is to use.

In this chapter, we will be covering the following topics:

- Creating a simple HTML page
- Adding jQuery Mobile to the page
- Updating the HTML to make use of the data attributes jQuery Mobile recognizes

Important preliminary points

You can find all the source code for this chapter in the c1 folder of the ZIP file you downloaded from GitHub. If you wish to type everything out by hand, we recommend you to use similar filenames.

Building an HTML page

Let's begin with a simple web page that is not mobile-optimized. To be clear, we aren't saying it can't be viewed on a mobile device. Not at all! But it may not be *usable* on a mobile device. It may be hard to read (the text may be too small). It may be too wide. It may use forms that don't work well on a touchscreen. We don't know the kinds of problems we will face until we start testing (and we've all tested our websites on mobile devices to see how well they work, right?).

Let's have a look at Listing 1-1:

```
Listing 1-1: test1.html
<html>
  <head>
    <title>First Mobile Example</title>
  </head>
  <body>
    <h1>Welcome</h1>
    <p>
    Welcome to our first mobile web site. It's going to be the
    best site you've ever seen. Once we get some content. And a
    business plan. But the hard part is done!
    </p>
    <p>
    <i>Copyright Megacorp &copy; 2015</i>
    </p>
  </body>
</html>
```

As we said, it isn't too complex, right? Let's take a quick look at this in the browser:

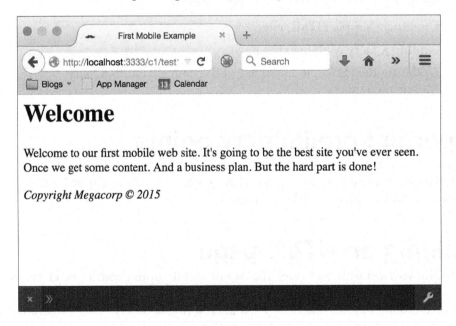

Not so bad, right? But let's take a look at the same page in a mobile simulator:

Wow, the text is in a barely readable font size. You've probably seen web pages like this before on your mobile device. You can, of course, typically use pinch and zoom or double-click actions to increase the size of the text. But it would be preferable to have the page render immediately in a mobile-friendly view. This is where jQuery Mobile enters.

Getting jQuery Mobile

In the preface, we talked about how jQuery Mobile is *just* a set of files. This wasn't said to minimize the amount of work done to create those files or to play down how powerful they are, but to emphasize that using jQuery Mobile means that you don't have to install any special tools or server. You can download the files and simply include them in your page. And if that's too much work, you have an even simpler solution. jQuery Mobile's files are hosted on a **Content Delivery Network (CDN)**. This is a resource hosted by them and it is guaranteed (as much as anything like this can be) to be online and available. Multiple websites are already using these CDN hosted files. This means that when users hit your website, they may already have the resources in their cache. For this book, we will be making use of the CDN hosted files. Just for this first example, we'll download the ZIP file and extract the files we need.

 I recommend doing this anyway for the times when you're on an airplane and wanting to whip up a quick mobile website.

To grab the files, visit `http://jquerymobile.com/download`. There are a few options here, but you want the **ZIP file** option. Go ahead and download the ZIP file and extract it (the ZIP file you downloaded earlier from GitHub has a copy already). The following screenshot demonstrates what you should see after extracting the content from the ZIP file:

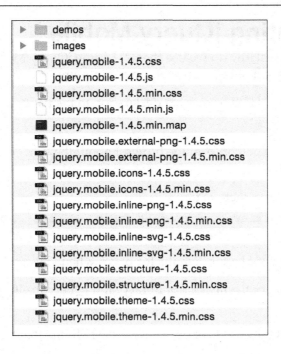

 An important note: at the time this book was written, jQuery Mobile was at version 1.4.5. Obviously, by the time you read this book, a later version may be released. The filenames you see listed in the previous screenshot are version-specific, so keep in mind that they may look a bit different for you.

The ZIP file contains `demos` and both the minified and regular versions of the jQuery Mobile framework. Additional files are provided for theming and other purposes, but your main concern will be with `jquery.mobile-1.4.5.min.css` and `jquery.mobile-1.4.5.min.js`. You will typically want to use the minified version in your production apps though. The `images` folder contains various images used by jQuery Mobile's CSS file. Of course, you also need to include the jQuery library.

 You can download this separately at `http://www.jquery.com`.

Implementing jQuery Mobile

Ok, we've got the bits. How do we use them? Adding jQuery Mobile support to a website requires the following three steps at a minimum:

1. First, add the HTML5 DOCTYPE declaration to the page:

   ```
   <!DOCTYPE html>
   ```

   This is used to help inform the browser about the type of content it will be dealing with

2. Add a viewport meta tag:

   ```
   <meta name="viewport" content="width=device-width, initial-
   scale=1">
   ```

   This will help set better defaults for pages when viewed on a mobile device

3. Finally, the CSS, the JavaScript library, and jQuery itself need to be included into the file.

Let's look at a modified version of our previous HTML file that adds all of these:

```
Listing 1-2: test2.html
<!DOCTYPE html>
<html>
  <head>
    <title>First Mobile Example</title>
    <meta name="viewport" content="width=device-width, initial-
      scale=1">
    <link rel="stylesheet" href="jquery.mobile-1.4.5.min.css" />
    <script type="text/javascript"
      src="http://code.jquery.com/jquery-2.1.3.min.js"></script>
    <script type="text/javascript" src="jquery.mobile-1.4.5.min.js"></
script>
  </head>
  <body>
    <h1>Welcome</h1>
    <p>
      Welcome to our first mobile web site.
      It's going to be the best site you've ever seen.
      Once we get some content. And a business plan.
      But the hard part is done!
    </p>
    <p>
      <i>Copyright Megacorp &copy; 2015</i>
    </p>
  </body>
</html>
```

For the most part, this version is the exact same as `listing 1`, except for the addition of the `DOCTYPE` declaration, the CSS link, and our two JavaScript libraries. Notice that we pointed to the hosted version of the jQuery library. It's perfectly fine to mix local JavaScript files and remote ones. If you want to ensure that you can work offline, you can simply download the jQuery library as well.

So, while nothing changed in the code between the body tags, there is going to be a radically different view now in the browser. The following screenshot shows how the iOS mobile browser renders the page now:

Right away, you see a couple of differences. The biggest difference is the relative size of the text. Notice how much bigger and easier to read it is. As we said, the user could have zoomed in on the previous version, but many mobile users aren't aware of this technique. This page loads up immediately in a manner that is much more usable on a mobile device.

Working with data attributes

As we saw in the previous example, just adding in jQuery Mobile goes a long way to updating our page for mobile support. But there's a lot more involved to really prepare our pages for mobile devices. As we work with jQuery Mobile over the course of the book, we're going to use various data attributes to mark up our pages in a way that jQuery Mobile understands. But what are data attributes?

HTML5 introduced the concept of data attributes as a way to add ad hoc values to the **Document Object Model (DOM)**. As an example, this is a perfectly valid HTML:

```
<div id="mainDiv" data-ray="moo">Some content</div>
```

In the previous HTML, the `data-ray` attribute is completely made up. However, because our attribute begins with `data-`, it is also completely legal. So, what happens when you view this in your browser? Nothing! The point of these data attributes is to integrate with other code, like JavaScript that does whatever it wants with them. So, for example, you could write JavaScript that finds every item in the DOM with the `data-ray` attribute and change the background color to whatever was specified in the value.

This is where jQuery Mobile comes in, making extensive use of data attributes both for markup (to create widgets) and behavior (to control what happens when links are clicked). Let's look at one of the main uses of data attributes within jQuery Mobile—defining pages, headers, content, and footers:

```
Listing 1-3: test3.html
<!DOCTYPE html>
<html>
<head>
<title>First Mobile Example</title>
<meta name="viewport" content="width=device-width, initial-scale=1">
<link rel="stylesheet" href="jquery.mobile-1.4.5.min.css" />
<script type="text/javascript" src="http://code.jquery.com/jquery-
2.1.3.min.js"></script>
```

```
<script type="text/javascript" src="jquery.mobile-1.4.5.min.js"></
script>
</head>

<body>

<div data-role="page">

    <div data-role="header"><h1>Welcome</h1></div>

    <div role="main" class="ui-content">
    <p>
    Welcome to our first mobile web site.
      It's going to be the best site you've ever seen.
    Once we get some content. And a business plan.
      But the hard part is done!
    </p>
    </div>

    <div data-role="footer">
    <h4>Copyright Megacorp &copy; 2015</h4>
    </div>

</div>

</body>
</html>
```

Compare the previous code snippet to `listing 1-2` and you will see that the main difference was the addition of the `div` blocks. One `div` block defines the page. Notice that it wraps all of the content inside the `body` tags. Inside the `body` tag, there are three separate `div` blocks. One has a role of `header`, another a role of `content`, and the final one is marked as `footer`. The `header` and `footer` blocks use `data-role`, which should give you a clue that we're defining a role for each of the blocks. The center `div` block, the one for `content`, uses the `role` attribute instead of `data-role` and adds a class. This is a special exception where jQuery Mobile (most recently) has switched to using a class directly to help speed up the initial layout of the page. As we stated earlier, these data attributes mean nothing to the browser itself, but jQuery Mobile can recognize them and enhance them.

Let's look at the new version of the page:

Notice right away that both the header and footer now have a gray background applied to them. This makes them stick out even more from the rest of the content. Speaking of content, the page text now has a bit of space between it and the sides. The header and footer were enhanced automatically by the jQuery Mobile JavaScript library, while the use of the `ui-class` style on the main content made use of the CSS provided with the framework. This is a theme you will see repeated again and again as we go through this book. A vast majority of the work you'll be doing will involve the use of data attributes or a bit of CSS.

Summary

In this chapter, we talked a bit about how web pages may not always render well in a mobile browser. We talked about how the simple use of jQuery Mobile can go a long way to improve the mobile experience of a website. Specifically, we discussed how you can download jQuery Mobile and add it to an existing HTML page, what data attributes mean in terms of HTML, and how jQuery Mobile makes use of data attributes to enhance your pages.

In the next chapter, we will build upon this usage and start working with links and multiple pages of content.

2
Working with jQuery Mobile Pages

In the previous chapter, you saw how easy it was to add jQuery Mobile to a simple HTML page. While it would be nice if every website consisted of one and only one page, real websites consist of multiple pages connected via links. jQuery Mobile makes it easy to work with multiple pages and provides many different ways to create and link them.

In this chapter, we will be covering the following topics:

- Adding multiple pages to one jQuery Mobile file
- How links are modified by jQuery Mobile (and how to disable it)
- How additional files can be linked and added to a jQuery Mobile website
- How jQuery Mobile automatically handles URLs to allow for easy bookmarking

Important preliminary points

As mentioned in the previous chapter, all of the code from this chapter is available via the ZIP file downloaded at GitHub.

Starting with this chapter, we will be presenting only the most relevant parts of each code listing. The first code listing will typically include all the code, while the later listings will focus on the important sections. Be sure to reference the complete code listings available via the downloaded ZIP file.

Adding multiple pages to one file

In the previous chapter, we worked on a file that had a simple page of text. For our first modification, we're going to add another page to the file and create a link to it. If you remember, jQuery Mobile looks for a particular `<div>` wrapper to help it know where your page is: `<div data-role="page">`. What makes jQuery Mobile so simple to use is that we can add another page by simply adding another `div` using the same format. The code snippet `Listing 2-1` shows a simple example of this feature:

```
Listing 2-1: test1.html
<!DOCTYPE html>
<html>
<head>
<meta name="viewport" content="width=device-width, initial-scale=1">
<title>Multi Page Example</title>
<link rel="stylesheet" href="http://code.jquery.com/mobile/1.4.5/
jquery.mobile-1.4.5.min.css" />
<script type="text/javascript" src="http://code.jquery.com/jquery-
2.1.3.min.js"></script>
<script type="text/javascript" src="http://code.jquery.com/
mobile/1.4.5/jquery.mobile-1.4.5.min.js"></script>
</head>

<body>

<div data-role="page" id="homePage">

    <div data-role="header"><h1>Welcome</h1></div>

    <div role="main" class="ui-content">
    <p>
    Welcome to our first mobile web site. It's going to be
     the best site you've ever seen. Once we get some content.
     And a business plan. But the hard part is done!
    </p>

    <p>
     You can also <a href="#aboutPage">learn more</a>
     about Megacorp.
    </p>
    </div>
```

```
    <div data-role="footer">
    <h4>Copyright Megacorp &copy; 2015</h4>
    </div>

</div>

<div data-role="page" id="aboutPage">

    <div data-role="header"><h1>About Megacorp</h1></div>

    <div role="main" class="ui-content">
    <p>
    This text talks about Megacorp and how interesting it is.
     Most likely though you want to <a href="#homePage">return</a>
     to the home page.
    </p>
    </div>

    <div data-role="footer">
    <h4>Copyright Megacorp &copy; 2015</h4>
    </div>

</div>
</body>
</html>
```

Okay! So, as always, we begin our template with a few required bits: the HTML5 DOCTYPE, the meta tag, one CSS file, and two JavaScript files. This was covered in the previous chapter and we will not be mentioning it again. Note that this template switches over to the CDN version of the CSS and JavaScript libraries:

```
<link rel="stylesheet" href="http://code.jquery.com/
  mobile/1.4.5/jquery.mobile-1.4.5.min.css" />
<script src="http://code.jquery.com/jquery-2.1.3.min.js"></script>
<script src="http://code.jquery.com/mobile/1.4.5/
  jquery.mobile-1.4.5.min.js"></script>
```

These versions are hosted by the jQuery team. Most likely, your visitors would have loaded these libraries already, so they exist in their cache before arriving at your mobile website. While this is the route we will take as we go further with our examples, remember that you can always use the version you downloaded instead.

Notice that we have two `<div>` blocks. The first hasn't changed much from the previous example. We've added a unique ID (`homepage`) as well as a second paragraph. Notice the link in the second paragraph. It's using a standard internal link (`#aboutPage`) to tell the browser that we want to simply scroll the browser down to that part of the page. The target specified, `aboutPage`, is defined right below in another `div` block.

In a traditional web page, this would be displayed as two main blocks of text on a page. Clicking any of the two links would simply scroll the browser up and down accordingly. However, jQuery Mobile is going to do something significantly different here. The following screenshot shows how the page is rendered in a mobile browser:

Notice something? Even though our HTML included two blocks of text (the two `<div>` blocks), it only rendered one. jQuery Mobile will always display the first page it finds and only that page. Here comes the best part. If you click on the link, the second page will automatically load. Using your device's back button or simply clicking on the link will return you back to the first page (obviously, this only works on devices that have a back button, for example, Android devices):

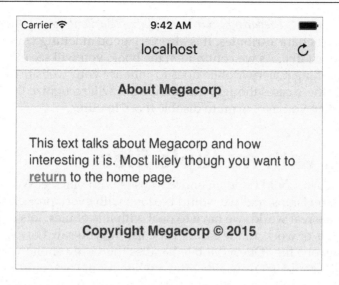

You will also notice a smooth transition. This is something you can configure later on. But all of the interactions here — the showing and hiding of pages and the transitions — were all done automatically by jQuery Mobile. Now is a good time to talk about links and what jQuery Mobile does when you click on them.

jQuery Mobile, links, and you

When jQuery Mobile encounters a simple link (`<a href="something.html">Foo</a>`), it will automatically capture any clicks on that link and change it to an AJAX-based load. This means that if it detects that the target is something on the same page, that is, the hashmark style (`href="#foo"`) links we used in the previous code, it will handle transitioning the user to a new page. If it detects a page to another file on the same server, it will use AJAX to load the page and replace the currently visible one.

If you link to an external website, then jQuery Mobile will leave the link as it is and the normal link behavior will occur. There may be times when you may want to disable jQuery Mobile from doing anything with your links at all. In this case, you can make use of a data attribute that lets the framework know it shouldn't do anything at all. Here is an example:

```
<a href="foo.html" data-ajax="false">Normal, non-special link</a>
```

As we saw in *Chapter 1, Preparing Your First jQuery Mobile Project*, jQuery Mobile makes heavy use of data attributes. It is also very good at letting you disable the behaviors you don't like. As we continue in the book, you will see example after example of something jQuery Mobile does to enhance your website for mobile devices. In all of these cases though, the framework will recognize that there may be times when you may want to disable those features.

Working with multiple files

In an ideal world, we could build an entire website with one file. We would never have to perform revisions, and we would be done with every project by 2 P.M. on Fridays. But in the real world, we have to deal with lots of files, lots of revisions, and, unfortunately, lots of work. In the earlier code listing, you saw how we could include two pages within one file. jQuery Mobile handles this easily enough. But you can imagine that this would get unwieldy after a while. While we could include 10, 20, or even 30 pages, this will make the file difficult to work with and make the initial download for the user that much slower.

To work with multiple pages and files, all we need to do is make a simple link to other files in the same domain as our first file. We can even combine the first technique (two pages in one file) with links to the other files. In listing 2-2, we've modified the first example to add a link to a new page (as mentioned previously, we are only listing the relevant portion of the page):

```
Listing 2-2:test2.html
<div data-role="page" id="homePage">

    <div data-role="header"><h1>Welcome</h1></div>

    <div role="main" class="ui-content">
    <p>
    Welcome to our first mobile web site. It's going to be
    the best site you've ever seen. Once we get some content.
    And a business plan. But the hard part is done!
    </p>

    <p>
    Find out about our wonderful
    <a href="products.html">products</a>.
    </p>
```

```
     <p>
     You can also <a href="#aboutPage">learn more</a>
     about Megacorp.
     </p>
     </div>

     <div data-role="footer">
     <h4>Copyright Megacorp &copy; 2015</h4>
     </div>

   </div>

   <div data-role="page" id="aboutPage">

     <div data-role="header"><h1>About Megacorp</h1></div>

     <div role="main" class="ui-content">
     <p>
     This text talks about Megacorp and how interesting it is.
      Most likely though you want to <a href="#homePage">return</a>
      to the home page.
     </p>
     </div>

     <div data-role="footer">
     <h4>Copyright Megacorp &copy; 2015</h4>
     </div>

   </div>
```

Now, let's look at `listing 2-3`, our **Products** page:

```
Listing 2-3: products.html
<!DOCTYPE html>
<html>
<head>
<meta name="viewport" content="width=device-width, initial-scale=1">
<title>Products</title>
<link rel="stylesheet" href="http://code.jquery.com/mobile/1.4.5/
jquery.mobile-1.4.5.min.css" />
<script type="text/javascript" src="http://code.jquery.com/jquery-
2.1.3.min.js"></script>
```

```
<script type="text/javascript" src="http://code.jquery.com/
mobile/1.4.5/jquery.mobile-1.4.5.min.js"></script>
</head>

<body>

<div data-role="page" id="productsPage">

  <div data-role="header"><h1>Products</h1></div>

  <div role="main" class="ui-content">
  <p>
  Our products include:
  </p>
  <ul>
    <li>Alpha Series</li>
    <li>Beta Series</li>
    <li>Gamma Series</li>
  </ul>
  </div>


</div>

</body>
</html>
```

Our **Products** page is rather simple, but notice that we included the jQuery and jQuery Mobile resources on top. Why? I mentioned earlier that jQuery Mobile is going to use AJAX to load your additional pages. If you open `test2.html` in any modern browser, you can see this for yourself using developer tools. Clicking on the link for **Products** will fire an **XML HTTP Request** (**XHR**), but generally, it just means an AJAX call, as shown in the following screenshot from Chrome's DevTools:

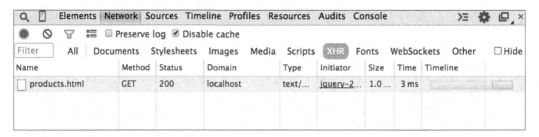

That's neat. But what happens when someone bookmarks the application? Let's now take a look at how jQuery Mobile handles URLs and navigation.

What are browser developer tools?

All modern browsers have built-in tools to help you build web pages. These tools allow you to inspect and manipulate the DOM, pause and debug JavaScript execution, and view network activity and errors.

jQuery Mobile and URLs

If you've opened `test2.html` in your browser and played with it, you may have noticed something interesting about the URLs as you navigate. The following is the initial `http://localhost/mobile/c2/test2.html` URL (the address and folder will, of course, differ on your computer).

After clicking on **Products**, the URL will change to `http://localhost/mobile/c2/products.html`. If I click on back and click on **learn more**, I will get `http://localhost/mobile/c2/test2.html#aboutPage`.

In both the subpages (the **Products** page and the **About** page), the URL was changed by the framework itself. The framework uses `history.pushState` and `history.replaceState` in the browsers that support it. For older browsers, or browsers that don't support JavaScript manipulation of the URL, hash-based navigation is used instead. The `http://localhost/mobile/c2/test2.html#/mobile/c2/products.html` URL is an example of how this link would look.

What's interesting is that, in this bookmark style, `test2.html` is always loaded first. You could actually build your `products.html` file to only include `div` and be assured that if the request was made for products first, it would still render correctly. It's the newer and fancier browsers that have an issue. If you didn't include the proper jQuery and jQuery Mobile includes, when they go directly to `products.html`, you would end up with a page that has no styles. It's best to simply always include your proper header files (the CSS, the JavaScript, and so on). Any decent editor will provide simple ways to create templates.

Additional customization

Working with multiple pages in jQuery Mobile is pretty simple. You could take what's been discussed in the first two chapters and build a pretty simple, but mobile-compliant, website right now. The following are a few more interesting tricks you may want to consider.

Page titles

You may have noticed that when you clicked on the **Products** page in the previous example, the title of the browser correctly updated to **Products**. This is because jQuery Mobile noticed, and parsed in, the `title` tag from the `products.html` file. If you click on the **learn more** link, you will notice that the title is also updated. How did this work? When `aboutPage` was loaded, jQuery Mobile used the `header` tag's content (**All About Megacorp**) for a title. You can override this by providing an additional argument to your `div` tag defining your page: `data-title`. The following snippet demonstrates this feature:

```
<div data-role="page" id="aboutPage" data-title="All About Megacorp">
    <div data-role="header"><h1>About Megacorp</h1></div>
```

You can find this version in `test3.html`.

Prefetching content

The benefit of including all your content within one HTML file is that all of your pages will be available immediately. But the negatives (too difficult to update and too slow for an initial download) far outweigh this. Most jQuery Mobile applications will include multiple files and typically just use one or two pages per file. You can, however, ensure speedier loading of some pages to help improve the user experience. Imagine our **Megacorp** website. It's got three pages, but the **Products** page is a separate HTML file. Since it's the only real content on the website, all of our users will most likely end up clicking on this link. We can tell jQuery Mobile to prefetch the content immediately upon the main page loading. This way, when the user does click on the link, the page will load much quicker. Once again, this comes down to one simple data attribute:

```
<p>
    Find out about our wonderful <a href="products.html" data-
        prefetch="true">products</a>.
</p>
```

In the previous link, all we've done is added `data-prefetch="true"` to the link. When jQuery Mobile finds this in a link, it will automatically fetch the content right away. Now, when the user clicks on the **Products** link, they will see the content even quicker. This modification is saved in `test4.html`.

Obviously, this technique should be used with care. Given a page with four main links, you may want to consider only prefetching the two most popular pages, not all four.

Changing page transitions

Earlier, we mentioned that you could configure the transitions jQuery Mobile uses between pages. Later in the book, we'll discuss how to do this globally. But if you want to switch to a different transition for a particular link, just include a `data-transition` attribute in your link:

```
<p>
Find out about our wonderful <a href="products.html" data-
  transition="pop">products</a>.
</p>
```

Valid values for transition include `fade` (the default), `flip`, `flow`, `pop`, `slide`, `slidedown`, `slidefade`, `turn`, and `none`.

Many transitions also support a reverse action. Normally, jQuery Mobile figures out if you need this, but if you want to force a direction, use the `data-direction` attribute:

```
<p>
Find out about our wonderful <a href="products.html" data-
  transition="pop" data-direction="reverse">products</a>.
</p>
```

Summary

This chapter further fleshed out the concept of jQuery Mobile pages and how to work with multiple pages. Specifically, we saw how one physical file can contain many different pages. jQuery Mobile will handle hiding all but the first page. We also saw how you can link to other pages and how jQuery Mobile uses AJAX to dynamically load the content into the browser. Next, we discussed how jQuery Mobile handles updating the URL of the browser in order to enable bookmarking. Finally, we discussed two utilities that will help to improve your page. The first way was to provide a title for embedded pages. The second technique demonstrated how to prefetch content to further improve the experience of the users visiting your website.

In the next chapter, we'll take a look at headers, footers, and navbars. These will greatly enhance our pages and make them easier to navigate.

3
Enhancing Pages with Headers, Footers, and Toolbars

Toolbars provide a simple way to add navigation elements to a mobile website. They can be especially useful for consistent or website-wide navigation controls that users can always refer to when navigating through your application.

In this chapter, we will be covering the following topics:

- Talking about how to create both headers and footers
- Discussing how to turn these headers and footers into useful toolbars
- Demonstrating how to create fixed positioned toolbars that always show up no matter how large the content of a particular page is
- Showing an example of navigation bars

Important preliminary points

As mentioned in the previous chapter, all of the code from this chapter is available via the ZIP file downloaded at GitHub. The chapter will only consider the important parts of each file. Consult the downloaded files for the complete source.

Adding headers

You've already worked with headers in the previous chapter, so the code will be familiar. In this chapter, we will study them deeper and demonstrate how to add additional functionality, such as buttons, to your website headers.

If you remember, a `header` block can be defined by simply using a `div` tag with the appropriate role:

```
<div data-role="header"><h1>My Header</h1></div>
```

We can further add functionality to headers by adding buttons. Buttons could be used for navigation (for example, to return to the home screen) or to provide links to related pages. Because the center of the header is used for text, there are only two *spaces* available for buttons — one to the left and one to the right. Buttons can be added simply by creating links in your header. The first link will be to the left of the text and the second link to the right. The following file is an example:

```
Listing 3-1: header_test.html
<div data-role="header">
  <a href="index.html">Home</a>
  <h1>My Header</h1>
  <a href="contact.html">Contact</a>
</div>
```

When viewed in the mobile browser, you can see that the links were automatically turned into buttons:

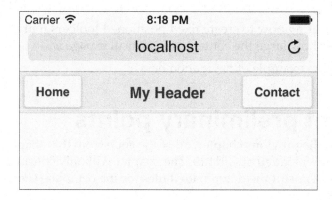

Notice how the simpler links were automatically turned into big buttons, making them easier to use and more *control-like* for the header. You may be wondering what if you only want one button on the right-hand side? Removing the first button and keeping the second in its place will not work, as shown in the following code snippet:

```
<div data-role="header">
  <h1>My Header</h1>
  <a href="contact.html">Contact</a>
</div>
```

The previous code snippet creates a button in the header but on the left-hand side. In order to position the button to the right, simply add the ui-btn-right class:

```
Listing 3-2: header_test2.html
<div data-role="header">
  <h1>My Header</h1>
  <a href="contact.html" class="ui-btn-right">Contact</a>
</div>
```

You can also specify ui-btn-left to place a link on the left-hand side, but as demonstrated in the previous code snippet, that's the normal behavior:

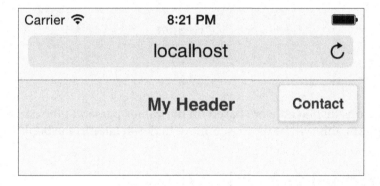

Icon sneak peek

While it is not specifically a header toolbar feature, one interesting feature available to all buttons in jQuery Mobile is the ability to specify an icon. A set of simple, easily recognizable icons ship with jQuery Mobile and are available to use immediately. These icons will be discussed further in *Chapter 6, Working with Forms and jQuery Mobile*. But as a quick preview, the following code snippet shows a header with two customized icons:

```
Listing 3-3: header_test3.html
<div data-role="header">
  <a href="index.html" data-icon="home">Home</a>
  <h1>My Header</h1>
  <a href="contact.html" data-icon="info">Contact</a>
</div>
```

Notice the new attribute, `data-icon`. When viewed in the browser, you will get what is shown in the following screenshot:

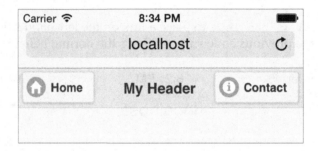

The specific icons displayed were based on the values passed to the `data-icon` attributes. Again, this will be discussed more in depth later in the book.

Working with back buttons

Depending on your user's hardware, they may or may not have a physical back button. For devices that do, such as Android phones, hitting the back button will work just fine in a jQuery Mobile application. Whichever page the user was on previously will be loaded as soon as the button is clicked. But on other devices, such as the iPhone, there is no such button to click. While you can provide links to navigate around pages yourself, jQuery Mobile provides some nice built-in support for navigating backwards out of the box.

There are two ways you can add an automatic back button. The code in `Listing 3-4` shows a simple two-page jQuery Mobile website. In the second page, we've added a new data attribute, `data-add-back-btn="true"`. This will create a **Back** button in the header of the second page automatically. Next, we also added a simple link in the page content. While the actual URL of the link is blank, make note of the `data-rel="back"` attribute. jQuery Mobile will detect this link and automatically send the user to the previous page:

```
Listing 3-4: back_button_test.html
<div data-role="page">

    <div data-role="header"><h1>My Header</h1></div>

    <div data-role="content">
    <p>
        <a href="#subpage">Go to the sub page...</a>
    </p>
    </div>

</div>

<div data-role="page" id="subpage" data-add-back-btn="true">
    <div data-role="header"><h1>Sub Page</h1></div>
    <div data-role="content">
      <p>
        <a href="" data-rel="back">Go back...</a>
      </p>
    </div>
    </div>
```

The following screenshot demonstrates the feature in action:

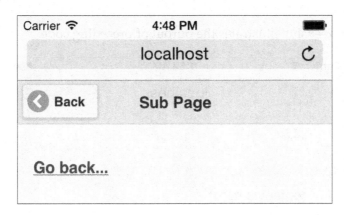

In case you're curious, the text of the button can be customized by simply using another data attribute in your page div: `data-add-back-btn="true" data-back-btn-text="Return"`. You can turn on the **Back** button support globally and change the text via JavaScript as well. This will be discussed in *Chapter 9, jQuery Mobile Configuration, Utilities, and JavaScript Methods*.

As a final example, what if you want to create a header without any actual text? Imagine for a moment that you include this header:

```
<div data-role="header">
        <a href="index.html" data-icon="home">Home</a>
</div>
```

When viewed in the mobile browser, the header is not properly sized because it is missing the `<h1>` tag normally used to provide text:

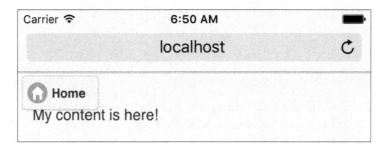

Luckily, there is a simple fix for this. Add a span tag with the `ui-title` class to the header and all will be fine:

```
<div data-role="header">
    <a href="index.html" data-icon="home">Home</a>
    <span class="ui-title"></span>
</div>
```

The following screenshot illustrates the output of preceding code:

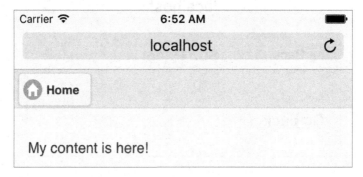

Working with footers

Footers are going to be, for the most part, much like headers. We previously demonstrated the use of `data-role` to create a footer:

```
<div data-role="footer"><h4>My Footer</h4></div>
```

As with headers, you can include buttons in the footer. Unlike headers, the buttons in a footer do not automatically position themselves to the left and right of the text. Rather, they simply line up from the left-hand side. The following is a simple example with two buttons:

```
<div data-role="footer">
  <a href="credits.html">Credits</a>
  <a href="contact.html">Contact</a>
</div>
```

The following screenshot demonstrates this feature:

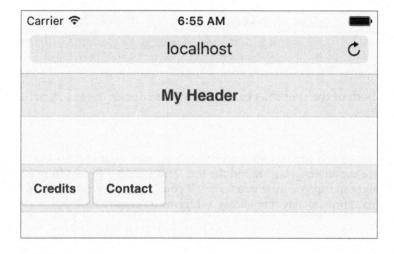

This works, but note that the buttons don't have much space around them. You can improve this by adding a class called `ui-bar` to your footer `div` tag, as shown in the following code snippet:

```
<div data-role="footer" class="ui-bar">
  <a href="credits.html">Credits</a>
  <a href="contact.html">Contact</a>
</div>
```

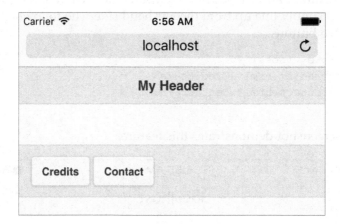

You can find both of the previous examples in the `footer_test2.html` and `footer_test3.html` files.

 Note that if you include footer text along with your buttons, you should *not* use an `<h4>` tag around the text. This is a bit different from headers and can trip you up if you forget. If you do forget, your header will end up approximately three times as high as it needs to be.

Creating fixed and fullscreen headers and footers

In the previous discussion about headers and footers, you saw a few examples on how buttons can be added. These buttons could be useful to navigate in your website. But what if a particular page is somewhat long? A blog entry, for example, could be quite long, especially when viewed on a mobile device. As the user scrolls, the header or footer could be offscreen. jQuery Mobile provides a way to create fixed position headers and footers.

With this feature enabled, the header and footer will always be visible. In a page with long content, the user can scroll up and down, but the headers and footers will remain in their proper positions. This only works with mobile browsers that support the `fixed` value for the CSS `position` property. For browsers that do not support this feature, the headers and footers will act normally. This feature can be enabled by adding `data-position="fixed"` to the `div` tag used for either the header or the footer. The code in `Listing 3-5` demonstrates this example. In order to ensure that the page actually scrolls, many paragraphs of text were repeated. This has been removed from the code in the book, but exists in the actual file:

```
Listing 3-5: longpage.html
<div data-role="page">
    <div data-role="header" data-position="fixed"><h1>My
       Header</h1></div>

    <div data-role="content">
      <p>
        Lorem ipsum dolor sit amet, consectetur adipiscing elit.
           Suspendisse id posuere lacus. Nulla ac sem ut eros
           dignissim interdum a et erat. Class aptent taciti
           sociosqu ad litora torquent per conubia nostra, per
           inceptos himenaeos. In ac tellus est. Nunc consequat
           parturient montes, nascetur ridiculus mus. In id
           lectus.Quisque mauris ipsum, vehicula id ornare aliq
           auctor volutpat dui. Sed euismod sem in arcu dapibus
           condimentum dictum nibh consequat.
      </p>
    </div>

    <div data-role="footer" data-position="fixed"><h4>My
       Footer</h4></div>
    </div>
```

Here is a screenshot of the feature in action where the page was scrolled down a bit:

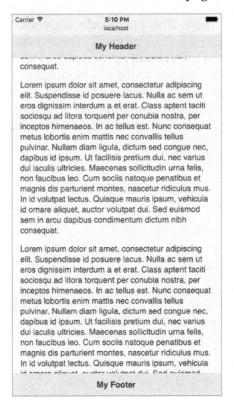

Fullscreen headers and footers

Another option to consider is what's called fullscreen headers and footers. This is a metaphor commonly used with pictures, but it can also be used where fixed-positioned headers and footers are used. In this scenario, the header and footer appear and disappear with clicks. So, with a photo, this gives you a view of the photo as it is and also the ability to get the header and footer back with a simple click. Perhaps, instead of fullscreen headers or footer, you can consider it as *retrievable* headers and footers. In general, this is best used when you want the content of the page to be viewed by itself—again, an excellent example of this would be pictures.

To enable this feature, simply add `data-fullscreen="true"` to the `header` and `footer` tags in a page (yes, you can choose to enable fullscreen support for only the header or the footer if you wish). The code in `Listing 3-6` demonstrates this feature:

```
Listing 3-6: fullscreen.html
<div data-role="page">
```

```
<div data-role="header" data-position="fixed"
     data-fullscreen="true"><h1>My Header</h1>
</div>

<div role="content" class="ui-content">
  <p>
    <img src="green.png" title="Green Block">
  </p>
</div>

<div data-role="footer" data-position="fixed"
     data-fullscreen="true"><h4>My Footer</h4>
</div>

</div>
```

Here is how the page is rendered at first:

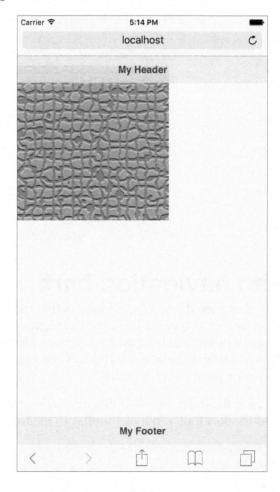

Here it is after the page is clicked and the image takes full priority in the page's view:

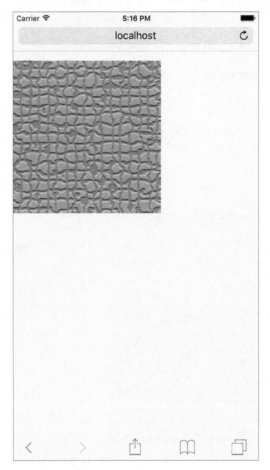

Working with navigation bars

You've now seen a few examples of headers and footers that include buttons, but jQuery Mobile has a cleaner version of this called **navigation bars (navbars)**. These are fullscreen-wide bars used to hold buttons. jQuery Mobile also supports highlighting one button at a time as an active button. When used for navigation, this is an easy way to mark a page as being active.

A navbar is simply an unordered list wrapped in a `div` tag that uses `data-role="navbar"`. Placed inside a footer, it looks similar to the following code snippet:

```
<div data-role="footer">
    <div data-role="navbar">
```

```
    <ul>
      <li><a href="header_and_footer__with_navbar.html"
      class="ui-btn-active">Home</a></li>
      <li><a
      href="header_and_footer__with_navbar_credits.html"
      >Credits</a></li>
      <li><a href="header_and_footer__with_navbar_contact.html"
      >Contact</a></li>
    </ul>
  </div>
</div>
```

Notice the use of `class="ui-btn-active"` in the first link. This will mark the first button as active. jQuery Mobile won't be able to do this for you automatically, so as you build each page and make use of `navbar`, you will have to *move* the class appropriately. The following screenshot shows how it looks:

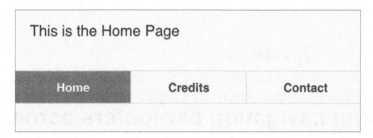

You can add up to five buttons and jQuery Mobile will appropriately size the buttons to make them fit. If you go over five, then the buttons will simply be split over multiple lines. Most likely, this is not something you want to cover. Overwhelming the user with too many buttons is a sure way to confuse, and ultimately anger, your users.

You can also include `navbar` in your header. If placed after the text or any other buttons, jQuery Mobile will automatically drop it to the next line:

```
<div data-role="header">
  <h1>Home</h1>
  <div data-role="navbar">
    <ul>
      <li><a href="header_and_footer_with_navbar.html" class="ui-
btn-
        active">Home</a></li>
      <li><a href="header_and_footer_with_navbar_credits.html"
>Credits</a></li>
```

```
        <li><a href="header_and_footer_with_navbar_contact.html"
>Contact</a></li>
      </ul>
    </div>
  </div>
```

You can see an example of both of these in action in the file named `header_and_footer_with_navbar.html`:

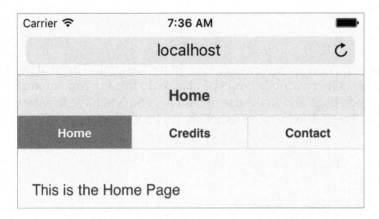

Persisting navigation bar footers across multiple pages

Let's now take two of the previous topics and combine them into one incredibly cool little feature—multiple page persistent footers. It needs a bit more work, but you can create a footer `navbar` that will not disappear when switching from page to page. In order to do this, you have to follow a few simple rules:

- Your footer `div` must be present on all the pages
- Your footer `div` must use the same `data-id` value across all the pages
- You should use the CSS classes `ui-btn-active` on the *active* page in `navbar`
- The footer has to specify a theme, and the same theme, across all the pages
- You must also use the persistent footer feature

That sounded a bit complex, but it's really just a tiny bit more HTML in your template. In `listing 3-7`, an index page for a fictional company makes use of a footer navbar. Note the use of `ui-state-persist` and `ui-btn-active` for the currently selected page:

```
Listing 3-7: persistent_footer_index.html
```

```
<div data-role="footer" data-position="fixed"
    data-id="footernav" data-theme="a">
  <div data-role="navbar">
    <ul>
      <li>
        <a href="persistent_footer_index.html"
          class="ui-btn-active">Home</a>
      </li>
      <li>
        <a href="persistent_footer_credits.html">Credits</a>
      </li>
      <li>
        <a href="persistent_footer_contact.html">Contact</a>
      </li>
    </ul>
  </div>
</div>
```

The following screenshot shows how the complete page looks:

We don't need to worry so much about the other two pages. You can find them in the ZIP file you downloaded. The following code snippet is the footer section for the second page. Notice that the only change here is the movement of the `ui-btn-active` class:

```
<div data-role="footer" data-position="fixed"
               data-id="footernav" data-theme="a">
  <div data-role="navbar">
    <ul>
      <li>
        <a href="persistent_footer_index.html">Home</a>
      </li>
      <li>
        <a href="persistent_footer_credits.html"
           class="ui-btn-active">Credits</a>
      </li>
      <li>
        <a href="persistent_footer_contact.html">Contact</a>
      </li>
    </ul>
  </div>
</div>
```

Clicking from one page to another shows a smooth transition to each page, but the footer bar remains. Much like a framed website (don't shudder; frames weren't always looked at with scorn), the footer will stay as the user navigates throughout the website.

Summary

In this chapter, we discussed how to add headers, footers, and navbars to your jQuery Mobile pages. We showed how the proper `div` tags will create nicely formatted headers and footers on your page, and how to make these headers and footers persist over a long page. Furthermore, we demonstrated *fullscreen mode* for headers and footers. These are headers and footers that appear and disappear with clicks—perfect for images and other items you want to show in a fullscreen type view on your mobile device. Finally, we saw how to combine persistent footers and navbars to create a footer that doesn't go away when the page changes.

In the next chapter, we'll dive deep into lists. Lists are one of the primary ways folks add navigation and menus to their mobile websites. jQuery Mobile provides a plethora of options for creating and styling lists.

4
Working with Lists

Lists are a great way to provide menus to users on a mobile website. They take content and focus it down into smaller chunks that the brain can easily consume one bite at a time. jQuery Mobile provides a wealth of list options, from simple lists to lists with custom thumbnails and multiple user actions.

In this chapter, we will be covering the following topics:

- How to create lists
- How to create linked and submenu-style lists
- How to create different styles of lists

Creating lists

As you've (hopefully!) come to learn, jQuery Mobile takes an approach of *enhancement* when it comes to UI. You take ordinary, simple HTML and add a bit of markup (sometimes!), and jQuery Mobile will do the heavy lifting of enhancing the UI. The same process applies to lists. We've all worked with simple lists in HTML before; the following code snippet is an example:

```
<ul>
  <li>Raymond Camden</li>
  <li>Scott Stroz</li>
  <li>Todd Sharp</li>
  <li>Dave Ferguson</li>
</ul>
```

We all know how they are displayed (a bulleted list in the case of the previous code snippet). Let's take that list and drop it in a simple jQuery Mobile-optimized page. The code in Listing 4-1 takes a typical page and drops in our list:

```
Listing 4-1: test1.html
  <div data-role="page">
    <div data-role="header">
      <h1>My Header</h1>
    </div>
    <div role="main" class="ui-content">
        <ul>
            <li>Raymond Camden</li>
            <li>Scott Stroz</li>
            <li>Todd Sharp</li>
            <li>Dave Ferguson</li>
        </ul>
    </div>
    <div data-role="footer">
      <h1>My Footer</h1>
    </div>
  </div>
```

Given this HTML, jQuery Mobile gives us something good right away, as shown in the following screenshot:

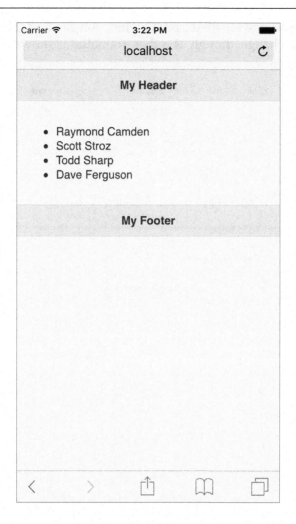

We can enhance that list though with a simple change. Take the ordinary `<ul>` tag from `Listing 4-1` and add a `data-role="listview"` attribute, as shown in the following line of code:

```
<ul data-role="listview">
```

In the code which you downloaded from GitHub, you can find this modification in test2.html. The change, though, is rather dramatic, as shown in the following screenshot:

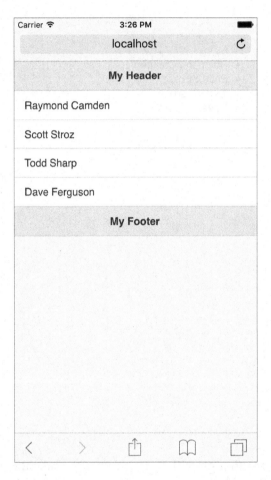

You can see that the items no longer have the bullets in front, but they are much larger and easier to read. Things get even more interesting when we begin to add links to our list. In the following code snippet, I've added a link to each list item:

```
<ul data-role="listview">
  <li><a href="ray.html">Raymond Camden</a></li>
  <li><a href="scott.html">Scott Stroz</a></li>
  <li><a href="todd.html">Todd Sharp</a></li>
  <li><a href="dave.html">Dave Ferguson</a></li>
</ul>
```

Once again, you can find the complete file this was taken from in the ZIP file you downloaded earlier. This one may be found in `test3.html`. The following screenshot shows how this code was rendered:

Notice the new arrow image. This was automatically added when jQuery Mobile detected a link in your list. Now, you've turned a relatively simple HTML unordered list into a simple menu system. This, by itself, is pretty impressive; but as we will see throughout the remaining chapter, jQuery Mobile provides a wealth of rendering options to let you customize your lists.

Working with list features

jQuery Mobile provides multiple different styles of lists as well as different features that can be applied to them. For the next part of this chapter, we'll cover some (but not all!) of these available options. These aren't in any particular order and are presented as a gallery of options available to you. You probably will not (and should not!) try to use all of these within one application, but it's good to keep in mind the various types of list styles available via jQuery Mobile.

Creating inset lists

One of the simplest and slickest changes you can make to your lists is to turn them into **inset lists**. These are lists that do not take up the full width of the device. Taking the initial list we modified with `data-role="content"`, we can simply add another attribute, `data-inset="true"`, to the following code block (found in `test4.html`):

```
<ul data-role="listview" data-inset="true">
  <li>Raymond Camden</li>
  <li>Scott Stroz</li>
  <li>Todd Sharp</li>
  <li>Dave Ferguson</li>
</ul>
```

The result is now very different from the earlier example, as shown in the following screenshot:

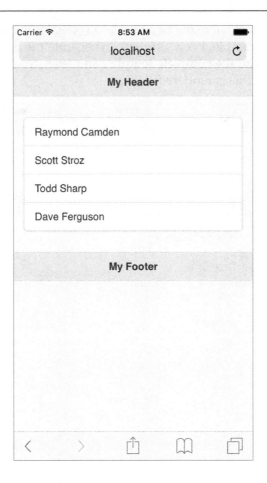

Creating list dividers

Another interesting UI element you may wish to add to your lists is **dividers**. These are a great way to separate a long list into something that is a bit easier to scan. Adding a list divider is as simple as adding a `li` tag that makes use of `data-role="list-divider"`. The following code snippet shows a simple example of this element:

```
<ul data-role="listview" data-inset="true">
  <li data-role="list-divider">Active</li>
  <li>Raymond Camden</li>
  <li>Scott Stroz</li>
  <li>Todd Sharp</li>
  <li data-role="list-divider">Archived</li>
  <li>Dave Ferguson</li>
</ul>
```

In the previous code block, note the two new `li` tags making use of the `list-divider` role. In this example, I've used these to separate the list of people into two groups. You can find the complete template in `test5.html`. The following screenshot shows how this is rendered:

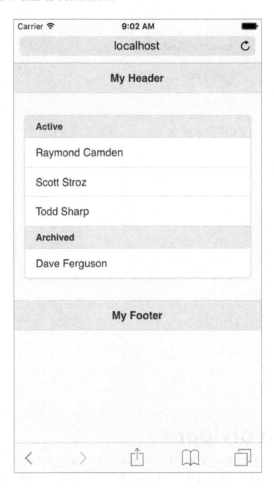

Autodividers

Another option for dividers is to have jQuery Mobile create them for you automatically. By adding `data-autodividers="true"` to any listview, jQuery Mobile automatically divides lists by the first letter of the item (you can tweak this with custom JavaScript if you wish). Here's an example of a simple list with autodividers (from `test6.html`):

```
<ul data-role="listview" data-inset="true"
data-autodividers="true">
```

```
    <li>Apples</li>
    <li>Apricots</li>
    <li>Bananas</li>
    <li>Cherries</li>
    <li>Coconuts</li>
</ul>
```

Notice that there are no dividers in the list, but that `autodividers` is enabled at the top level of the list itself. This creates the following in the browser:

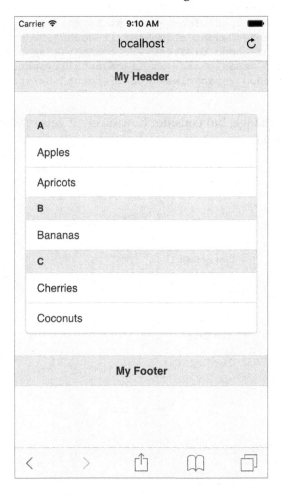

If you were to add a new list item, let's say for donuts, `listview` will automatically add a new **D** divider. And let's be honest—no list is complete without donuts.

Creating lists with count bubbles

Yet another interesting UI trick you can perform with jQuery Mobile lists are **count bubbles**. This is a UI enhancement that adds a simple number to the end of each list item. The numbers are wrapped in a *bubble-like* look, which is commonly used for e-mail style interfaces. In the following code snippet, the count bubble is used to signify the number of cookies consumed at a technical conference. This number is supplied inside a span tag that uses a class of `ui-li-count`:

```
<ul data-role="listview" data-inset="true">
   <li data-role="list-divider">Cookies Eaten</li>
   <li>Raymond Camden <span class="ui-li-count">9</span></li>
   <li>Scott Stroz <span class="ui-li-count">4</span></li>
   <li>Todd Sharp <span class="ui-li-count">13</span></li>
   <li>Dave Ferguson <span class="ui-li-count">8</span></li>
</ul>
```

It is a simple HTML change, but consider how nicely it gets rendered, as shown in the following screenshot:

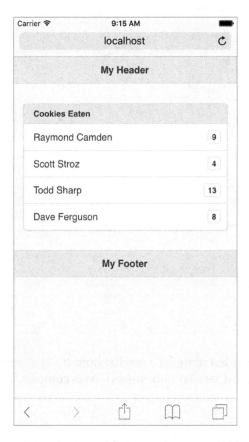

You can find a complete example of this feature in `test7.html`.

Using thumbnails and icons

Another common need with lists is to include images. jQuery Mobile supports both thumbnails (smallish images) and icons (even smaller images) that display well within the list's control. Let's first look at including thumbnails within your list. Assuming you already have nicely-sized images (our examples are all 160 pixels wide by 160 pixels high), you can simply include them within each `li` element, as demonstrated in the following code snippet:

```
<ul data-role="listview" data-inset="true">
  <li><a href="ray.html"><img src="ray.png"> Raymond Camden</a></li>
  <li><a href="scott.html"><img src="scott.png"> Scott Stroz</a></li>
  <li><a href="todd.html"><img src="todd.png"> Todd Sharp</a></li>
  <li><a href="dave.html"><img src="dave.png"> Dave Ferguson</a></li>
</ul>
```

Nothing special is done with the image; no data attribute or class is added. jQuery Mobile will automatically align the image to the left and the item text to the top of each `li` block:

You can find the previous demonstration in `test8.html`. So, what about icons? To include an icon in your code, add the `ui-li-icon` class to your image (note that the beginning of the class is `ui`, not `ul`). The following code snippet is an example of this with the same list:

```
<ul data-role="listview" data-inset="true">
    <li>
        <a href="ray.html">
            <img src="ray_small.png" class="ui-li-icon">
            Raymond Camden
        </a>
    </li>
    <li>
        <a href="scott.html">
            <img src="scott_small.png" class="ui-li-icon">
            Scott Stroz
        </a>
    </li>
    <li>
        <a href="todd.html">
            <img src="todd_small.png" class="ui-li-icon">
            Todd Sharp
        </a>
    </li>
    <li>
        <a href="dave.html">
            <img src="dave_small.png" class="ui-li-icon">
            Dave Ferguson
        </a>
    </li>
</ul>
```

jQuery Mobile does shrink images when used with this class, but in my experience, the formatting is better when the image is resized beforehand. Doing so also improves the speed of your web page as smaller images should result in quicker download times. The preceding screenshots are all 16 pixels wide and high. The result is as follows:

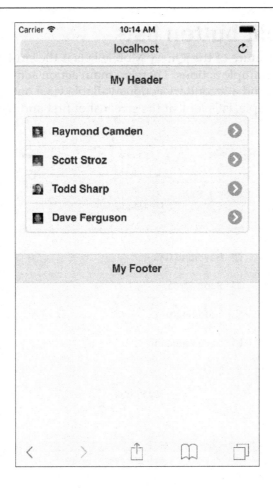

You can find the previous example in `test9.html`.

Creating split button lists

Another interesting feature of the jQuery Mobile lists is the **split button list**. This is simply a list with multiple actions. There's a main action activated when the user clicks on the list item and a secondary action available via a button at the end of the list item. For this example, let's look at the screenshot first and then show how it's done:

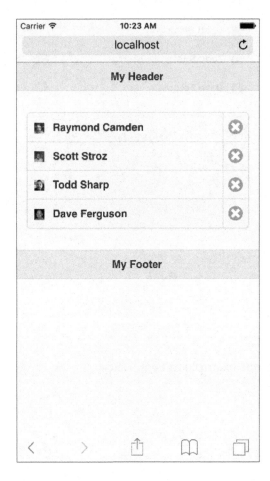

As you can see, each list item has a secondary icon at the end of the row. This is an example of a split item list and it is defined by simply adding a second link to a list item, for example:

```
<ul data-role="listview" data-inset="true">
    <li>
        <a href="ray.html">
            <img src="ray_small.png" class="ui-li-icon">
```

```
                    Raymond Camden
                </a>
                <a href="foo.html">Delete</a>
        </li>
        <li>
            <a href="scott.html">
                <img src="scott_small.png" class="ui-li-icon">
                Scott Stroz
            </a>
            <a href="foo.html">Delete</a>
        </li>
        <li>
            <a href="todd.html">
                <img src="todd_small.png" class="ui-li-icon">
                Todd Sharp
            </a>
            <a href="foo.html">Delete</a></li>
        <li>
            <a href="dave.html">
                <img src="dave_small.png" class="ui-li-icon">
                Dave Ferguson
            </a>
            <a href="foo.html">Delete</a>
        </li>
    </ul>
```

Note that the second link's text, Delete, is actually replaced by the icon. You can specify an icon by adding the data attribute split-icon to your ul tag, as shown in the following line of code:

```
<ul data-role="listview" data-inset="true" data-split-icon="delete">
```

The complete code for this example may be found in test10.html.

Summary

This chapter discussed how to work with list views in jQuery Mobile. We saw how to turn a regular HTML list into a mobile-optimized list, and we demonstrated the numerous types of list features available with the framework.

In the next chapter, we'll take what we've learned already and build a real (albeit a bit simple) mobile-optimized website for a hotel.

5

Getting Practical – Building a Simple Hotel Mobile Website

In the past four chapters, we looked at a few features of jQuery Mobile. But we already have enough knowledge to build a simple, pretty basic mobile-optimized website.

In this chapter, we will be covering the following topics:

- Discussing what our hotel mobile website will contain
- Creating the hotel's mobile website using jQuery Mobile
- Discussing what could be done to make the website more interactive

Welcome to Hotel Camden

The Hotel Camden, known throughout the world, has had a web presence for some time now (okay, just to be clear, we're making this up!). They were an early innovator in the online world, beginning with a simple website in 1996 and gradually improving their online presence over the years. Online visitors to Hotel Camden can now see virtual tours of the rooms, check the grounds with a stunning 3D Adobe Flash plugin, and actually make reservations online. Recently, though, the owners of Hotel Camden decided that they want to move into the mobile space. For now, they want to start simply by creating a mobile-optimized website that includes the following features:

- **Contact information**: This will include both a phone number and an e-mail address. Ideally, the user will be able to click on these and get connected to a real person.
- **Map of the hotel location**: This should include the address and possibly a map too.

- **Room types available**: This can be a simple list of the rooms from the simplest to the grand ones.
- **Provide a way for the user to get to the real website**: We are accepting that our mobile version will be somewhat limited (for this version), so at a minimum, we should provide a way for users to return to the desktop version of the website.

The home page

Let's begin with the initial home page for the Camden Hotel. This will provide a simple list of options as well as a bit of marketing text at the top. The text doesn't actually help anyone, but the marketing staff won't let us release the website without it:

```
Listing 5-1: index.html
<!DOCTYPE html>
<html>
  <head>
  <title>The Camden Hotel</title>
  <meta name="viewport"
      content="width=device-width, initial-scale=1">
  <link rel="stylesheet"
  href="http://code.jquery.com/mobile/1.4.5/jquery.mobile-1.4.5.min.
css" />
  <script type="text/javascript"
  src="http://code.jquery.com/jquery-2.1.3.min.js">
  </script>
  <script type="text/javascript"
  src="http://code.jquery.com/mobile/1.4.5/jquery.mobile-1.4.5.min.
js">
  </script>
  </head>
  <body>
    <div data-role="page">
      <div data-role="header">
        <h1>Camden Hotel</h1>
      </div>
      <div role="main" class="io-content">
        <p>
```

```
       Welcome to the Camden Hotel. We are a luxury hotel
         specializing in catering to the rich and overly
         privileged. You will find our accommodations both
         flattering to your ego, as well as damaging to your
         wallet. Enjoy our complimentary wi-fi access, as well as
         caviar baths while sleeping in beds with gold thread.
       </p>
       <ul data-role="listview" data-inset="true">
         <li><a href="find.html">Find Us</a></li>
         <li><a href="rooms.html">Our Rooms</a></li>
         <li><a href="contact.html">Contact Us</a></li>
         <li><a href="">Non-Mobile Site</a></li>
       </ul>
     </div>
     <div data-role="footer">
       <h4>&copy; Camden Hotel 2016</h4>
     </div>
   </div>
 </body>
</html>
```

At a high level, the code in `listing 5-1` is simply another instance of the jQuery page model that we've discussed before. You can see what the CSS and JavaScript include as well as the `div` wrappers that set up your page, header, footer, and content. Within your content `div`, you can also see a list being used. We've left the URL blank for the `Non-Mobile Site` option as we don't have a real website for the Camden Hotel.

The order of the list items is also thought through. Each item is listed in the order the staff feels is the most commonly requested with number one being simply finding the hotel and the last option (to ignore leaving the website) being contacting the hotel.

Overall, the idea of this example is to provide quick access to the most important aspects of what we think hotel customers will need. The following screenshot shows how the website looks:

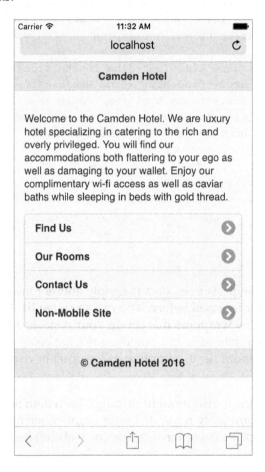

It isn't terribly exciting, but it renders well and is easy to use. Later on, you'll learn how to theme jQuery Mobile, so your website doesn't look like every other example out there.

Finding the hotel

The next page of our mobile website is focused on helping the user find the hotel. This will include the address as well as a map. The code in Listing 5-2 shows how this is done (as a reminder, we are saving space and trimming the code samples a bit):

```
Listing 5-2: find.html
<div data-role="page">
    <div data-role="header">
      <h1>Find Us</h1>
    </div>
    <div role="main" class="ui-content">
      <p>
        The Camden Hotel is located in beautiful downtown
        Lafayette, LA. Home of the Ragin Cajuns, good food, good
        music, and all around good times, the Camden Hotel is
        smack dab in the middle of one of the most interesting
        cities in America!
      </p>
      <p>
        400 Kaliste Saloom<br/>
        Lafayette, LA<br/>
        70508
      </p>
      <p>
        <img src="http://maps.googleapis.com/maps/api/
          staticmap?center=400+Kaliste+Saloom, +Lafayette,
          LA&zoom=12&size=150x150&scale=2&maptype=roadmap&
          markers=label:H%7C400+Kaliste+Saloom, +Lafayette,
          LA&sensor=false">
      </p>
    </div>
    <div data-role="footer">
      <h4>&copy; Camden Hotel 2016</h4>
    </div>
</div>
```

The beginning of the template has our boilerplate included again, and as before, we have some marketing speak fluff on top. Immediately below this though are the address and the map. We created the map using one of the cooler Google features, **Static Maps**. You can read more about Google Static Maps at `http://code.google.com/apis/maps/documentation/staticmaps/`. Essentially, it is a way to create static maps via URL parameters. There's no zooming or panning in these maps. But if you are just trying to show a user where your business is located, it's an incredibly powerful and simple way to do so. Unlike the traditional Google Maps API, which is driven by JavaScript, the Static Maps API is simply an image URL with URL parameters specifying options for size, location, and other factors. While there are a large number of options you can use with this API, our example simply centers it on an address and adds a marker there as well. The address used is simply one in my home town and does not reflect a real business. The label **H** is used for the marker, but a custom icon could be used instead. The following screenshot shows how this looks:

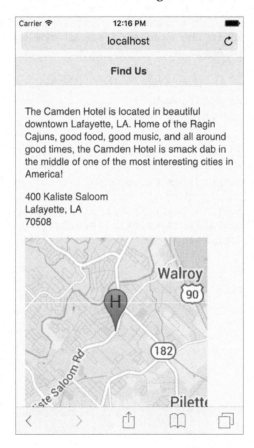

You could play around with this map URL a bit more to change the zoom, colors, and so on to your liking.

Listing the hotel rooms

Now let's look at rooms.html. This is where we will list out the room types available at the hotel:

```
Listing 5-3: rooms.html
<div data-role="page">
    <div data-role="header">
      <h1>Our Rooms</h1>
    </div>
    <div role="main" class="ui-content">
      <p>
        Select a room below to see a picture.
      </p>
      <ul data-role="listview" data-inset="true">
        <li><a href="room_poor.html">Simple Elegance</a></li>
        <li><a href="room_medium.html">Gold Standard</a></li>
        <li><a href="room_high.html">Emperor Suite</a></li>
      </ul>
    </div>
    <div data-role="footer">
      <h4>&copy; Camden Hotel 2016</h4>
    </div>
</div>
```

The rooms page is simply a list of rooms. The hotel has three levels of rooms, each linked to from the list so that the user can get its details. You can find all three files in the ZIP file downloaded from GitHub. Let's look at one of them in detail:

```
Listing 5-4: room_high.html
<div data-role="page" data-fullscreen="true">
    <div data-role="header" data-position="fixed">
      <h1>Emperor Suite</h1>
    </div>
    <div data-role="content">
      <img src="room2.jpg" />
    </div>
    <div data-role="footer" data-position="fixed">
      <h4>&copy; Camden Hotel 2012</h4>
    </div>
</div>
```

The room detail page is only an image. It is not very helpful, but it gets the point across. However, notice that we used a trick we learned in *Chapter 3, Enhancing Pages with Headers, Footers, and Toolbars*: the fullscreen mode. This allows the user to quickly click and hide the headers, so they can see the room in all its glory:

Contacting the hotel

Now let's take a look at the contact page. This will provide the user with information on how to reach the hotel:

```
Listing 5-5: contact.html
<div data-role="page">
    <div data-role="header">
      <h1>Contact Us</h1>
    </div>
    <div role="main" class="ui-content">
      <p>
        <b>Phone:</b> <a href="tel:555-555-5555">
          555-555-5555</a><br/>
```

```
        <b>Email:</b> <a href="mailto:people@camdenhotel.fake">
            people@camdenhotel.fake</a>
        </p>
    </div>
    <div data-role="footer">
        <h4>&copy; Camden Hotel 2012</h4>
    </div>
</div>
```

As before, we've wrapped our page in the proper script blocks and `div` tags. Make a special note of our two links. Both the **Phone** and **E-mail** links use URLs that may not look familiar to you. The first, `tel:555-555-555`, is actually a way to ask the mobile device to call a phone number. Clicking on it brings up the dialer, as shown in the following screenshot:

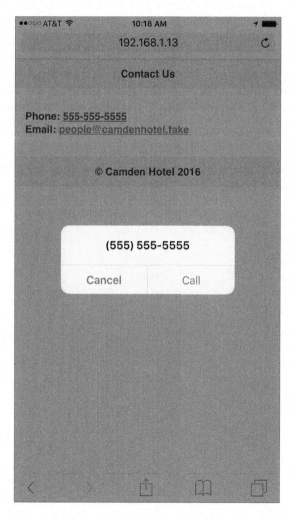

This makes it easy for the user to quickly call the hotel. Similarly, the `mailto` link will allow you to quickly jot an e-mail off to the hotel. Other URL schemes exist, including ones to send an SMS message. As you can probably guess, this scheme uses the form `sms`. So, to begin an SMS message to a phone number, you could use the `sms://5551112222` URL.

For additional examples, consider the official documentation for iOS URL schemes (`http://developer.apple.com/library/ios/#featuredarticles/iPhoneURLScheme_Reference/Introduction/Introduction.html`). Most of these should work just fine on Android as well. For a good overview of other platforms, the HTML5 Mobile Development DZone Reference Card is an excellent resource (`http://refcardz.dzone.com/refcardz/html5-mobile-development`).

Summary

In this chapter, we took what we've learned so far and built a very simple, but effective, website for a fake hotel. This website shared essential information for folks needing to learn about the hotel while on a mobile device. We made use of Google's Static Maps API to create a simple map showing the hotel's location and demonstrated the use of `tel` and `mailto` URL schemes for automatic phone dialing and e-mailing.

In the next chapter, we'll take a look at forms and how they are automatically improved with jQuery Mobile.

6
Working with Forms and jQuery Mobile

In this chapter, we will look at forms. Forms are a critical part of most websites, as they provide the primary way for users to interact with the website. jQuery Mobile goes a long way to ward making forms both usable and elegantly designed for mobile devices.

In this chapter, we will be covering the following topics:

- Talking about what jQuery Mobile does with forms
- Working with a sample form and describing how results are handled
- Discussing specifics about how to build certain types of forms and making use of jQuery Mobile conventions

Before you begin

In this chapter, we're going to talk about forms and how jQuery Mobile enhances them. As a part of our discussion, we will be posting our forms to a local server. To process forms, you need a type of application server. They could be written in PHP, Node.js, Ruby, and so on. Since that is outside the scope of our book, we're simply going to post to a static HTML file. Keep in mind that you can process forms posted from a jQuery Mobile website *exactly* like you would for any other form.

What jQuery Mobile does with forms

Before we get into the code, there are two very important things you should know about what jQuery Mobile will do with your HTML forms. They are as follows:

- All the forms will submit their data via Ajax. This means that the data will be sent directly to the action of your form and the result will be brought back to the user and placed within the page that held the form. This prevents a full page reload.

- All the form fields are automatically enhanced, each in its own way. As we go on in the chapter, you will see examples of this. But basically, jQuery Mobile modifies your form fields to work better on a mobile device. A great example of this is buttons. jQuery Mobile automatically widens and heightens buttons to make them easier to click in the small form factor of a phone. If for some reason, you don't like this, jQuery Mobile provides a way to disable this, either on a global or per-user basis.

- The final point to remember is that because jQuery Mobile loads pages into the view dynamically, you need to ensure that the ID values for all the form fields are unique across the website. So, in other words, you don't want two forms using a field with the ID of name. Instead, you want them to use something that is unique.

With these in mind, let's look at our first example in Listing 6-1:

```
Listing 6-1: test1.html
<div data-role="header">
    <h1>Form Demo</h1>
</div>
<div drole="main" class="ui-content">
    <form action="echo.html" method="post">
        <div class="ui-field-contain">
            <label for="name">Name:</label>
            <input type="text" name="name" id="name" value=""  />
        </div>
        <div class="ui-field-contain">
          <label for="email">Email:</label>
            <input type="text" name="email" id="email" value=""  />
        </div>
        <div class="ui-field-contain">
            <input type="submit" name="submit" value="Send"  />
        </div>
    </form>
</div>
```

As before, we focused on the important part of the template, the content within our main page `div` block. Notice that, for the most part, this is a generic form, but every label and field is wrapped with the following `div` block:

```
<div class="ui-field-contain">
</div>
```

This will help jQuery Mobile align the label and the form field. You'll see why in a moment. Our form has two text fields, one for name and one for e-mail. The last item is just the **Send** button. So, outside of using a particular class wrapper and ensuring we have labels for our form fields, nothing else special is going on here. Right away though, you can see some pretty impressive changes to the form, as shown in the following screenshot:

In the preceding screenshot you can notice how the labels are presented above the form fields. This gives the fields more space on mobile devices. Also, notice that the **Send** button is large and easy to click. If we rotate the device, jQuery Mobile will update the display to take advantage of the additional space:

Notice that the fields now line up directly to the right of their labels. So, what happens when the form is submitted? As mentioned at the beginning of this chapter, jQuery Mobile will automatically convert the form post into an AJAX-based form post. Your backend code would then process the form just like any other regular form. In the ZIP file containing this book's code, you'll find echo.html, which simply reports back a static message.

Another good example of how jQuery Mobile updates form fields is with textarea, which, by default, can be very difficult to work with on a mobile device, especially when the amount of text grows beyond the size of textarea and a scroll bar is added. In the following code listing, we've simply modified the previous form to include a third item, a **Bio** field that uses textarea. The complete file can be found in the book's code ZIP file as test2.html. The following code snippet is the div block added after the previous two fields:

```
<div class="ui-field-contain">
   <label for="bio">Bio:</label>
   <textarea name="bio" id="bio"></textarea>
</div>
```

When viewed on the device, `textarea` expands to take in more width like the regular text fields, and grows taller:

But once you begin typing and entering multiple lines of text, `textarea` automatically expands, as shown in the following screenshot:

This is much easier to read than using scroll bars. Now, let's look at another common form option—radio buttons and checkboxes.

Working with radio buttons and checkboxes

Both radio buttons and checkboxes are also updated to work nicely on a mobile device, but they require a little more code. In the earlier examples, we wrapped form fields with a `div` tag that made use of `data-role="fieldcontain"`. When working with radio buttons and checkboxes, one more tag is required:

```
<fieldset data-role="controlgroup">
```

This `fieldset` tag will be used to group together your radio buttons or checkboxes. The code in `Listing 6-3` demonstrates one set of radio buttons and one checkbox group:

```
Listing 6-3: test3.html
<div data-role="page">
        <div data-role="header">
          <h1>Form Demo</h1>
        </div>
        <div role="main" class="ui-content">
          <form action="echo.html" method="post">
<fieldset data-role="controlgroup">
              <legend>Favorite Movie:</legend>
              <input type="radio" name="favoritemovie"
                id="favoritemovie1" value="Star Wars">
              <label for="favoritemovie1">Star Wars</label>
              <input type="radio" name="favoritemovie"
                id="favoritemovie2" value="Vanilla Sky">
              <label for="favoritemovie2">Vanilla Sky</label>
              <input type="radio" name="favoritemovie"
                id="favoritemovie3" value="Inception">
              <label for="favoritemovie3">Inception</label>
</fieldset>
<fieldset data-role="controlgroup">
              <legend>Favorite Colors:</legend>
              <input type="checkbox" name="favoritecolor"
                id="favoritecolor1" value="Green">
              <label for="favoritecolor1">Green</label>
              <input type="checkbox" name="favoritecolor"
                id="favoritecolor2" value="Red">
              <label for="favoritecolor2">Red</label>
              <input type="checkbox" name="favoritecolor"
                id="favoritecolor3" value="Yellow">
              <label for="favoritecolor3">Yellow</label>
          </fieldset>
<input type="submit" name="submit" value="Send"  />
   </form>
        </div>
      </div>
```

Our form has two main questions: what is your favorite movie and what are your favorite colors? Each block is wrapped in the `div` tag we mentioned earlier. Inside this is `fieldset` using `data-role="controlgroup"`. Finally, you then have your radio and checkbox groups. It is important to include the labels with each input control as each of the previous examples has. Once rendered, jQuery Mobile will group these into a nice looking, singular control:

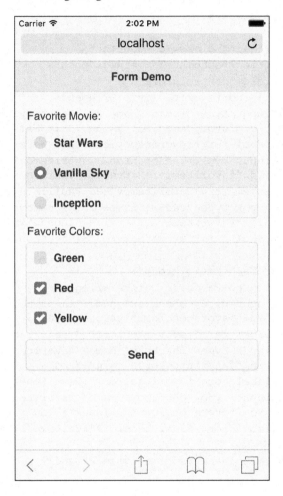

Notice the wide, clickable regions for each item. This makes it much easier to select items on a mobile device. Another interesting feature of both of these controls is the ability to turn them into horizontal button bars:

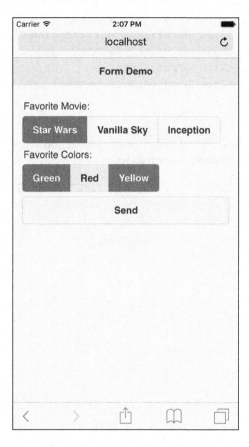

In `test4.html`, both the `fieldset` tags were modified to include a new data attribute:

```
<fieldset data-role="controlgroup" data-type="horizontal">
```

Working with select menus

Yet another example of jQuery Mobile form enhancement is with select menus. As with our earlier examples, we make use of a class on a `div` and a `label` tag, but outside of that, the `select` tag is used as normal.

The following code snippet is from `test5.html`:

```
<div class="ui-field-contain">
  <label for="favmovie">Favorite Movie:</label>
  <select name="favmovie" id="favmovie">
    <option value="Star Wars">Star Wars</option>
    <option value="Revenge of the Sith">Revenge of the Sith</option>
    <option value="Tron">Tron</option>
    <option value="Tron Legacy">Tron Legacy</option>
  </select>
</div>
```

On the mobile device, the initial display of the select control is modified to be easier to hit, as shown in the following screenshot:

However, once clicked, the device's native menu will take over. This will look different on the platform you are using. The following screenshot shows how iOS renders the menu:

Here is how Android renders it:

Another option to use with select fields is grouping. jQuery Mobile allows you to vertically or horizontally group together multiple select fields. In both the cases, all that's required is to wrap your select fields in `fieldset` using `data-role` of `controlgroup` much like we did earlier for radio buttons and checkboxes. The following code snippet is an example of a vertically aligned group of select fields:

```
<fieldset data-role="controlgroup">
    <legend>Trip Setup:</legend>
    <label for="location">Location</label>
    <select name="location" id="location">
      <option value="Home">Home</option>
      <option value="Work">Work</option>
      <option value="Moon">Moon</option>
      <option value="Airport">Airport</option>
    </select>
```

```
    <label for="time">Time</label>
    <select name="time" id="time">
      <option value="Morning">Morning</option>
      <option value="Afternoon">Afternoon</option>
      <option value="Evening">Evening</option>
    </select>
    <label for="time">Meal</label>
    <select name="meal" id="meal">
      <option value="Meat">Meat</option>
      <option value="Vegan">Vegan</option>
      <option value="Kosher">Kosher</option>
    </select>
  </fieldset>
```

The rest of this template can be found in `test6.html`. The following screenshot shows how it looks:

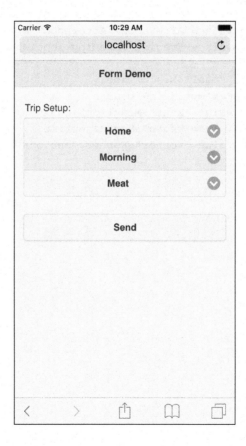

Note how jQuery Mobile groups them together and nicely rounds the corners. The horizontal version can be achieved by adding a `data-type="horizontal"` attribute to the `fieldset` tag. Here is an example (the complete file can be found in `test7.html`):

```html
<fieldset data-role="controlgroup" data-type="horizontal">
        <legend>Trip Setup:</legend>
        <label for="location">Location</label>
        <select name="location" id="location">
          <option value="Home">Home</option>
          <option value="Work">Work</option>
          <option value="Moon">Moon</option>
          <option value="Airport">Airport</option>
        </select>
        <label for="time">Time</label>
        <select name="time" id="time">
          <option value="Morning">Morning</option>
          <option value="Afternoon">Afternoon</option>
          <option value="Evening">Evening</option>
        </select>
        <label for="meal">Meal</label>
        <select name="meal" id="meal">
          <option value="Meat">Meat</option>
          <option value="Vegan">Vegan</option>
          <option value="Kosher">Kosher</option>
        </select>
      </fieldset>
```

The following screenshot shows the result:

Custom select fields

By default, jQuery Mobile only enhances the initial view of the select field, not the actual UI you get when clicking on the item to select an option. You can have a completely customized select UI by telling jQuery Mobile to not use *native* menus. This is done, of course, via another data attribute:

```
<select name="foo" data-native-menu="false">
```

A modified version of `test5.html` can be found in `test5-custom.html`. Look at how the control is modified when the user clicks on it:

In this case, the UI you see there will be consistent across all platforms.

Search, toggle, and slider fields

Along with taking regular form fields and making them work better, jQuery Mobile also helps make some of the newer HTML5 form fields work correctly across multiple browsers. While support still isn't nailed down on the desktop across every major browser, jQuery Mobile provides built-in support for search, toggle, and slider fields. Let's take a look at each of them.

Search fields

The simplest of the three new fields, search fields, simply adds a quick delete icon to the end of the field after you begin typing. Some devices will also put an hourglass icon in front to help convey the idea of the field being used for some types of search. To use this field, simply switch your type from `text` to `search`, as shown in the following example from `test8.html`:

```
<div class="ui-field-contain">
  <label for="name">Name:</label>
  <input type="search" name="name" id="name" value=""  />
</div>
```

The following screenshot is the result. Notice that I've typed a bit and the field has automatically added a delete icon at the end:

Flip switch fields

Flip switch fields are controls that flip back between one and two values. Creating a switch field involves using a checkbox control with a particular `data-role` value: `data-role="flipswitch"`. By default, the labels **On** and **Off** will be used for the switches, but you can customize the values by using the `data-on-text` and `data-off-text` attributes. Let's look at a simple example (you can find the complete source for this in `test9.html`):

```
<label for="test">Test:</label>
<input type="checkbox" data-role="flipswitch" name="test" id="test">

<label for="gender">Gender:</label>
<input type="checkbox" data-role="flipswitch" name="gender"
id="gender" data-off-text="Male" data-on-text="Female"
data-wrapper-class="custom-size-flipswitch">
```

This is how jQuery Mobile renders the switches:

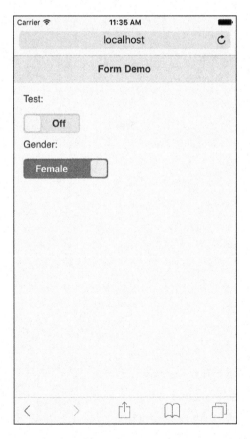

Unfortunately, you have to specify custom CSS when using your own labels. To fit **Male** and **Female** in the preceding example, the following CSS was used:

```css
.custom-size-flipswitch.ui-flipswitch .ui-btn.ui-flipswitch-on {
    text-indent: -5.9em;
}
.custom-size-flipswitch.ui-flipswitch .ui-flipswitch-off {
    text-indent: 0.5em;
}
/* Custom widths are needed because the length of custom labels
differs from
    the length of the standard labels */
.custom-size-flipswitch.ui-flipswitch {
    width: 8.875em;
}
.custom-size-flipswitch.ui-flipswitch.ui-flipswitch-active {
    padding-left: 7em;
    width: 1.875em;
}
@media (min-width: 28em) {
    // Repeated from rule .ui-flipswitch above
    .ui-field-contain > label + .custom-size-flipswitch.ui-flipswitch
{
        width: 1.875em;
    }
}
```

Slider fields

For the last of our special fields, we will take a look at sliders. Like search fields, they are based on an HTML5 specification that works in some browsers and not others. jQuery Mobile simply makes it work everywhere. To enable this field, we take a regular text field and switch `type` to `"range"`. jQuery Mobile supports two types of range controls—one with one simple slider and one with two sliders (for allowing a user to select a minimum and maximum value). Creating an enhanced slider control is as simple as using a `range` input type:

```html
<input type="range" name="coolness" id="coolness"
min="0" max="100" value="22" >
```

You can also add a highlight effect to `range` by using `data-highlight="true"`:

```html
<input type="range" name="something" id="something"
min="0" max="100" value="22" data-highlight="true">
```

You can find both of these in action in the file `test10.html`. Here is how they are rendered:

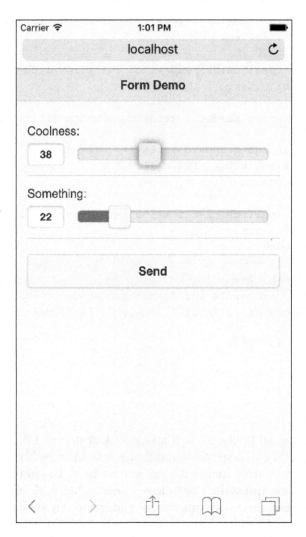

To give our slider a range, we also provide a `min` and a `max` value. You can also add additional color to the slider by adding the attribute: `data-highlight="true"`. The following code snippet is a sample (you can find the complete file in `test10.html`):

```
<div data-role="fieldcontain">
  <label for="coolness">Coolness:</label>
  <input type="range" name="coolness" id="coolness" min="0" max="100"
    value="22" data-highlight="true">
</div>
```

The support for the two range controls is provided by what jQuery Mobile refers to as a range slider. It is created with a `div` block and two input fields, as demonstrated in the following code:

```
<div data-role="rangeslider">
    <label for="coolnessLow">Cool Range:</label>
    <input type="range" name="coolnessLow" id="coolnessLow"
    min="0" max="100" value="22">
    <label for="coolnessHigh">Cool Range:</label>
    <input type="range" name="coolnessHigh" id="coolnessHigh"
    min="0" max="100" value="82">
</div>
```

Notice the `div` tag using the role of `rangeslider`. This is required along with both the range fields. You can find a complete demonstration in `test11.html`. The end result is one range control with two sliders, as shown in the following screenshot:

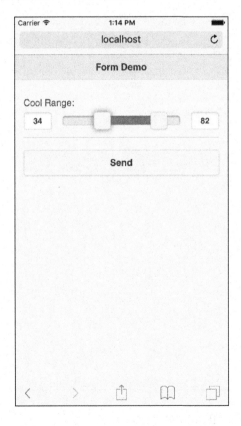

When posted to your form processor, you would use the first field value, `coolnessLow`, to represent the left range control and the second field value, `coolnessHigh`, to represent the second one.

Using native form controls

Now, you've seen how far jQuery Mobile will go to enhance and empower your form fields to work better on mobile devices. But what if you don't like what jQuery Mobile does? What if you love its updates to buttons, but despise its changes to dropdowns? Luckily, jQuery Mobile provides a simple way to disable automatic enhancement. In each field where you want to be left alone, simply add `data-role="none"` to the markup. So, given the following HTML, the first item will be updated while the second will not:

```
<input type="submit" value="Awesome">
<input type="submit" value="Not So Awesome" data-role="none">
```

Here's the output for the preceding code:

You can see an example of this in `test12.html`.

Another option is to disable it when jQuery Mobile is initialized. This option will be discussed in *Chapter 9, jQuery Mobile Configuration, Utilities, and JavaScript Methods*.

Working with mini fields

In the previous examples, we saw how jQuery Mobile automatically enhanced form fields to make them easier on smaller touch-based devices. In general, jQuery Mobile took your fields and made them nice and fat. While that's desirable most of the time, you may want to put your form fields on a bit of a diet. This is especially true for placing form fields in a header or footer. jQuery Mobile supports an attribute on any form field that creates a smaller version of the field: `data-mini="true"`. The following code snippet is a complete example:

```
<div class="ui-field-contain">
  <label for="name">Name:</label>
  <input type="search" name="name" id="name" value=""  />
</div>
<div class="ui-field-contain">
  <label for="name">Name (Slim):</label>
  <input type="search" name="name" id="name" value="" data-
    mini="true"  />
</div>
```

The result is a bit subtle, but you can see the height difference in the second field in the following screenshot:

This example may be found with the rest of the files in a file named `test13.html`.

Summary

In this chapter, we discussed forms and how they are rendered in a jQuery Mobile application. We discussed how jQuery Mobile automatically turns all the form submissions into AJAX-based calls and updates form fields to work better on mobile devices. Not only are all your form fields automatically updated, but you can also make use of new controls, such as the toggle, slider, and search inputs.

In the next chapter, we'll take a look at modal dialogs, widgets, and layout grids. These provide additional UI options for your mobile-optimized website.

7
Creating Grids, Panels, and Other Widgets

In this chapter, we will look at dialogs, grids, and other widgets. In the previous chapters, we dealt with pages, buttons, and form controls.

In this chapter, we will be covering the following topics:

- Demonstrating grids and how you can add them to your pages
- Showing how collapsible blocks allow you to pack a lot of information in a small amount of space
- Explaining how to create popups
- Discussing the responsive table and panel widgets
- Working with panels
- Using *filterable* widgets
- Adding *tabs*

Laying out content with grids

Grids are one of the few features of jQuery Mobile that do not make use of particular data attributes. Instead, you work with grids simply by specifying CSS classes for your content.

Grids come in four flavors: two-column, three-column, four-column, and five-column (you will probably not want to use the five-column one on a phone device. Save it for a tablet instead).

You begin a grid with a `div` block that makes use of the class `ui-grid-X`, where `X` will be either `a`, `b`, `c`, or `d`. The `ui-grid-a` class represents a two-column grid. The `ui-grid-b` class is a three-column grid. You can probably guess what `c` and `d` create.

So, to begin a two-column grid, you would have to wrap your content with the following code:

```
<div class="ui-grid-a">
   Content
</div>
```

Within the `div` tag, you then need to use `div` for each cell of the content. The class for grid calls begins with `ui-block-X`, where `X` goes from `a` to `d`. The `ui-block-a` class would be used for the first cell, `ui-block-b` for the next, and so on. This works much like the HTML tables.

Putting it together, the following code snippet demonstrates a simple two-column grid with two cells of content:

```
<div class="ui-grid-a">
  <div class="ui-block-a">Left</div>
  <div class="ui-block-b">Right</div>
</div>
```

The text within a cell will automatically wrap. The code in Listing 7-1 demonstrates a simple grid with a large amount of text in one of the columns:

```
Listing 7-1: test1.html
<div data-role="page" id="first">
     <div data-role="header">
       <h1>Grid Test</h1>
     </div>
     <div role="main" class="ui-content">
       <div class="ui-grid-a">
         <div class="ui-block-a">
         <p>
         This is my left hand content. There won't be a lot of
         it.
         </p>
         </div>
         <div class="ui-block-b">
           <p>
             This is my right hand content. I'm going to fill it
             with some dummy text.
           </p>
           <p>
```

```
      Bacon ipsum dolor sit amet andouille capicola spare
      ribs, short loin venison sausage prosciutto
      turkey flank frankfurter pork belly short ribs.
      chop, pancetta turkey bacon short ribs ham flank
      pork belly. Tongue strip steak short ribs tail
    </p>
   </div>
  </div>
 </div>
</div>
```

In the mobile browser, you can clearly see the two columns, as follows:

If the text in the `div` blocks seems a bit close together, there is a simple fix for it. To add a bit more space between the content of the grid cells, you can add a class to your main `div` that specifies `ui-content`. This tells jQuery Mobile to pad the content a bit, for example:

```
<div class="ui-grid-a ui-content">
```

This small change modifies the preceding screenshot as follows:

You can find this example in the file `test1-nicer.html`.

Working with other types of grids then is simply a matter of switching to the other classes. For example, a four-column grid would be set up similar to the following code snippet:

```
<div class="ui-grid-c">
  <div class="ui-block-a">1st cell</div>
  <div class="ui-block-b">2nd cell</div>
  <div class="ui-block-c">3rd cell</div>
</div>
```

Again, keep in mind your target audience. Anything over two columns may be too thin on a mobile phone.

To create multiple rows in a grid, you need to simply repeat the blocks. The following code snippet demonstrates a simple example of a grid with two rows of cells:

```
<div class="ui-grid-a">
  <div class="ui-block-a">Left Top</div>
  <div class="ui-block-b">Right Top</div>
  <div class="ui-block-a">Left Bottom</div>
  <div class="ui-block-b">Right Bottom</div>
</div>
```

Notice that there isn't any concept of a row. jQuery Mobile handles knowing that it should create a new row when the block starts over with the one marked `ui-block-a`. The code in `Listing 7-2`, is a simple example:

```
Listing 7-2:test2.html
<div data-role="page" id="first">
    <div data-role="header">
      <h1>Grid Test</h1>
    </div>
    <div role="main" class="ui-content">
      <div class="ui-grid-a">
        <div class="ui-block-a">
          <p>
            <img src="ray.png">
          </p>
        </div>
        <div class="ui-block-b">
        <p>
        This is Raymond Camden. Here is some text about him. It
        may wrap or it may not but jQuery Mobile will make it
        look good. Unlike Ray!
        </p>
        </div>
        <div class="ui-block-a">
          <p>
```

```
                This is Scott Stroz. Scott Stroz is a guy who plays
                golf and is really good at FPS video games.
            </p>
        </div>
        <div class="ui-block-b">
            <p>
                <img src="scott.png">
            </p>
        </div>
      </div>
    </div>
</div>
```

The following screenshot shows the result:

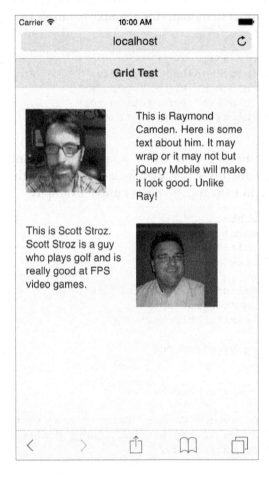

Making responsive grids

Earlier, in the chapter, we mentioned that complex grids may not work depending on the size of your targeted devices. A simple two-column grid is fine, but larger grids render well on tablets only. Luckily, there's a simple solution for it. jQuery Mobile's latest updates include much better support for responsive design. Let's consider a simple example. Here is a screenshot of a web page using a four-column grid:

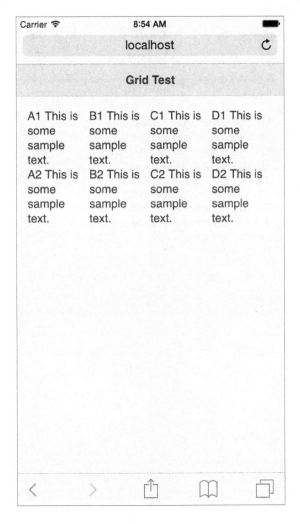

It's readable, but a bit dense. By making use of responsive design, we could handle the different sizes intelligently using the same basic HTML. jQuery Mobile enables a simple solution for this by adding the class `ui-responsive` to an existing grid. Here is an example:

```
<div class="ui-grid-c ui-responsive">
```

By making this one small change, look at how the phone version of our page changes in the following screenshot:

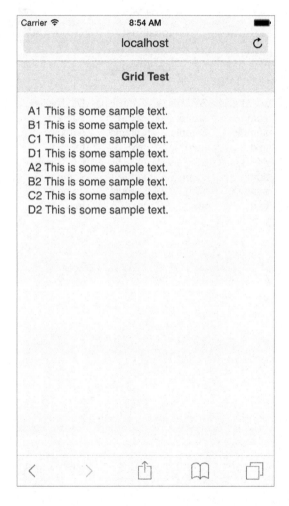

The four-column layout now is a one-column layout instead. If viewed on a tablet, the original four-column design will be preserved. You can find this example in `test4-r.html`.

Working with collapsible content

The next widget we will look at in this chapter supports collapsible content. This is simply the content that can be collapsed and expanded. Creating a collapsible content widget is as simple as wrapping it in a `div` block, adding `data-role="collapsible"`, and including a title for the content. Consider the following simple example:

```
<div data-role="collapsible">
  <h1>My News</h1>
  <p>This is the latest news about me…
</div>
```

Upon rendering, jQuery Mobile will turn the title into a clickable banner that can expand and collapse the content within. Let's look at a real example. Imagine you want to share the location of your company's primary address. You also want to include satellite offices. Since most people won't care about the other offices, we can use a simple collapsible content widget to hide the content by default. The following code snippet, `Listing 7-3`, demonstrates an example of this:

```
Listing 7-3: test5.html
    <div role="main" class="ui-content">

        <p>
        <strong>Main Office:</strong><br/>
        400 Elm Street<br/>
        New York, NY<br/>
        90210
        </p>

        <div data-role="collapsible">
            <h3>Satellite Offices</h3>

            <p>
            <strong>Asia:</strong>
            Another Address Here
            </p>

            <p>
            <strong>Europe:</strong>
            Another Address Here
            </p>

            <p>
            <strong>Mars:</strong>
```

```
            Another Address Here
            </p>

        </div>

    </div>
```

You can see that the other offices are all wrapped in the `div` tag using the new `collapsible` content role. When viewed, notice that they are hidden as follows:

Clicking on **+** next to the title opens it; it can be clicked again to close it, as shown in the following screenshot:

By default, jQuery Mobile will collapse and hide the content. You can, of course, tell jQuery Mobile to initialize the block open instead of closed. To do so, simply add `data-collapsed="false"` to the initial `div` tag. Take the following, for example:

```
<div data-role="collapsible" data-collapsed="false">
  <h1>My News</h1>
  <p>This is the latest news about me...
</div>
```

This region will still have the ability to collapse and open, but it will simply default to being opened initially.

Another option for `collapsible` content blocks is the ability to theme the content of the area that is collapsed. By providing a `data-content-theme` attribute, you can specify a background color that makes the region a bit more cohesive. Theming is covered in *Chapter 11, Enhancing jQuery Mobile*, but we can take a look at a quick example. In the following screenshot, the first region does not make use of the feature, while the second one does:

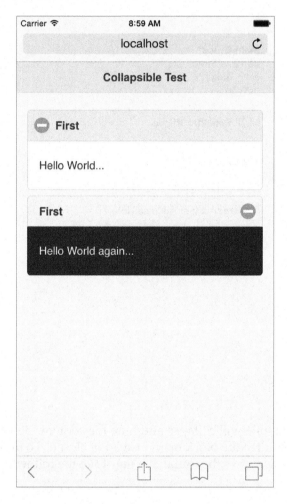

Notice that the icon is also shifted to the right. This demonstrates another option, `data-iconpos`. The following code snippet, found in the code folder as `test5-2.html`, demonstrates these options:

```
<div role="main" class="ui-content">
  <h3>First</h3>
  <p>
```

```
     Hello World...
   </p>
</div>
<div data-role="collapsible" data-content-theme="b"
     data-iconpos="right">
  <h3>First</h3>
  <p>
    Hello World again...
  </p>
</div>
```

Finally, you can take multiple collapsible regions and combine them
into one called an **accordion**. This is done by simply taking multiple collapsible
blocks and wrapping them in a new div tag. This div tag makes use of
data-role="collapsible-set" to make the inner blocks as one unit.
The code in Listing 7-6 demonstrates an example of this. It takes the earlier
office address example and uses a collapsible set for each unique address:

```
Listing 7-4: test6.html
<div data-role="page" id="first">
    <div data-role="header">
      <h1>Our Offices</h1>
    </div>
    <div role="main" class="ui-content">
      <div data-role="collapsible-set">
        <div data-role="collapsible">
          <h3>Main Office</h3>
            <p>
              400 Elm Street<br/>
              New York, NY<br/>
              90210
            </p>
        </div>
        <div data-role="collapsible">
          <h3>Asia</h3>
            <p>
              Another Address Here
            </p>
        </div>
        <div data-role="collapsible">
          <h3>Europe</h3>
            <p>
              Another Address Here
            </p>
        </div>
```

```
<div data-role="collapsible">
  <h3>Mars</h3>
    <p>
      Another Address Here
    </p>
</div>
  </div>
    </div>
      </div>
```

In listing 7-6, we simply wrap four collapsible blocks with a div tag that makes use of a collapsible set. Once done, jQuery Mobile will group them together and automatically close one when another is opened:

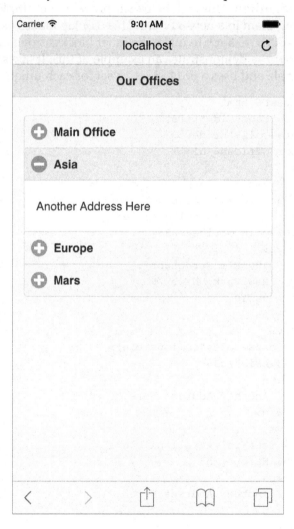

Using popups

Popups (also known as tooltips) are similar to dialogs, but they are much smaller and not necessarily modeled. They can be useful for providing contextual help or descriptive text.

Let's look at an example:

```
Listing 7-5: test7.html
<div data-role="page" id="first">

    <div data-role="header">
         <h1>Popup Demo</h1>
    </div>

    <div role="main" class="ui-content">

         <a href="#firstPopup" data-role="button"
data-rel="popup">Show Popup</a>

    </div>

    <div data-role="popup" id="firstPopup">
      <p>This is just a test. It has some text in it.
  It is incredibly awesome.</p>
    </div>

</div>
```

Inside our `main` content `div` is a simple link. In order to let jQuery Mobile know that this links to a popup, the `data-rel` attribute is specified. Note the ID value points to another `div` on the page. This `div` has the role of a popup. When viewed in the browser, jQuery Mobile automatically hides this div. It will only show up when the link is actually clicked:

As with the other widgets, you have multiple options you can specify for your popups. They include position options, modal properties, transitions (for opening and closing), and of course, theming. Let's look at position and modal properties, as they are the most interesting.

By default, popups will be positioned at the center of the item that launches them. So, for example, in our previous code listing, this was a button. You can modify this value by using a `data-position-to` attribute. The default is origin. You can center the popup to the entire window by using, you guessed it, window. Finally, you can also pass a jQuery selector as a value and that DOM item will be used to center the popup.

Normally, popups are dismissed if you click anywhere on the page. You can create a modal popup by setting it to be nondismissible. This is done by adding `data-dismissible="false"` to the `div` block containing the popup. To be clear, this is done to the `div` block, not the link. The code in `Listing 7-6` demonstrates an example of both these options:

```
Listing 7-6: test8.html
<div data-role="page" id="first">

    <div data-role="header">
        <h1>Advanced Popup Demo</h1>
    </div>

    <div role="main" class="ui-content">

        <a href="#firstPopup" data-role="button"
        data-rel="popup" data-position-to="window">
Show Popup</a>
        <p>
        I'm including some text here just so that we can
         properly demo the new position of my popup. It
         will be centered on the window, not the link
         above. That is <i>awesome</i>.
        </p>
    </div>

    <div data-role="popup" id="firstPopup" data-dismissible="false"
class="ui-content">
    <p>This is just a test. It has some text in it. It is incredibly
awesome.</p>
    <a href="" data-rel="back" data-theme="b" data-role="button">Get
Rid Of Me</a>
    </div>

</div>
```

This template is mostly like the previous one, but with a few important updates. First, take note of the `data-position-to` attribute. This will position the popup at the center of the window. We added some text to help make the page a bit taller in general. The next change was to the `popup` div. First, we added the `data-dismissible="false"` attribute to make it more of a modal dialog. In order to actually get rid of the popup, though, we have to add our own UI. To do this, we will add a button. By specifying `data-rel="back"`, jQuery Mobile will handle getting rid of the popup:

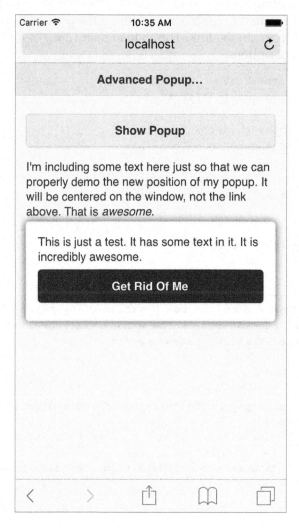

Responsive tables

Tables present a particular difficulty for mobile browsers. Generally, tables consist of a large amount of data. This could take up the entire screen of a desktop browser. On a mobile browser, this can be even more condensed. In the folder of this chapter's source code, take a look at `test_table.html`. We won't print the code here, but it is a rather simple four-column, four-row table. On a mobile device, this information will barely fit:

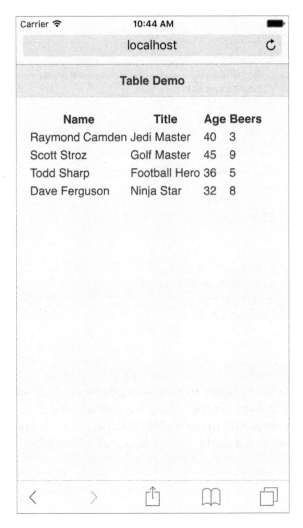

jQuery Mobile can make this work better by creating a responsive version of the table. There are a few small changes you must make to your tables to enable this feature. First, ensure your table makes use of the thead and tbody blocks. The previous example, test_table.html, did this already. The code in Listing 7-7 demonstrates what else we have to do to make the table responsive:

```
Listing 7-7: test_resp_table.html
<table data-role="table" id="table1" data-mode="reflow">
    <thead>
        <tr>
            <th>Name</th>
            <th>Title</th>
            <th>Age</th>
            <th>Beers</th>
        </tr>
    </thead>
    <tbody>
        <tr>
            <th>Raymond Camden</th>
            <td>Jedi Master</td>
            <td>40</td>
            <td>3</td>
        </tr>
        <tr>
            <th>Scott Stroz</th>
            <td>Golf Master</td>
            <td>45</td>
            <td>9</td>
        </tr>
    </tbody>
</table>
```

First, we add data-role="table" to the core table block. This will enable the basic responsive functionality for the table. Then, we will add the data-mode value to specify how the table responds to the mobile's display size. There is one more small change we will explain in a minute. Now take a look at the table:

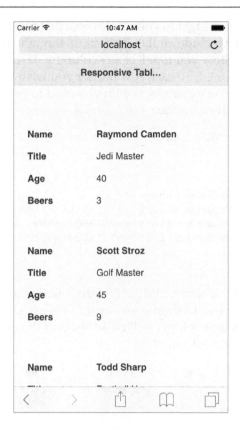

jQuery Mobile has broken the table up into blocks of content that are *much* easier to read. Even better, if you view this table on a larger screen tablet, it will render as a regular table. Remember the other change we mentioned? Note the vertical space between the first row (for **Raymond Camden**) and the second row (**Scott Stroz**). By default, jQuery Mobile will not add vertical spacing. This was accomplished by changing the first cell of each row to a `<th>` element. These elements are normally reserved for the top-level header, but they can be used inside `tbody` as well. For our demonstration here, they serve to help group the different rows in a more visually pleasing manner.

But wait, there's more! jQuery Mobile also supports another powerful feature: the ability to selectively filter the columns displayed to the user. The *column toggle* feature is enabled by adding `data-mode="columntoggle"` to a table. Take the following as an example:

```
<table data-role="table" data-mode="columntoggle" id="peopleTable"
class="ui-responsive">
```

This adds a column toggle widget to your table (note that for the button to associate with your table, you must include an ID). By default, though, the column toggle widget will not actually allow you to select any columns. To provide a list of columns, selectively add `data-priority` to each row header you wish to make toggle-enabled. You *do not* need to select every column, nor do you need to provide any specific order. Here's an example taken from the file `test_resp_adv_table.html`:

```
<table data-role="table" data-mode="columntoggle" id="peopleTable"
class="ui-responsive">
    <thead>
        <tr>
            <th>Name</th>
            <th data-priority="1">Title</th>
            <th data-priority="2">Age</th>
            <th data-priority="3">Beers</th>
        </tr>
    </thead>
```

Again, the order is totally arbitrary. While the order will probably match the order of your columns, you are free to choose any order you wish. Now, when the table is displayed, a column toggle widget will be added and the default display will be focused on the first priority column:

Clicking on the widget opens a popup:

The user can then select which columns they care about and the table will be updated automatically.

That's it! In case you're curious, you can change the text on the column toggle widget by simply using the attribute `data-column-btn-text` on the table.

Working with panels

The next widget we will discuss is the panel widget. The panel widget sits on the left- or right-hand side of your page and can be shown or hidden dynamically. Because of the limited real estate on mobile devices, panels are a nice way to hide navigation or other content until the user requests for them.

Creating a panel in jQuery Mobile is simple. First, add a new <div> block with data-role of panel. This must be done inside the div block that defines your page, and should be outside of the content region. The code in Listing 7-10 demonstrates an example of this:

```
Listing 7-8: test_panel.html
<div data-role="page" id="first">

    <div data-role="panel" id="leftPanel">
        This is the left panel.

        <p>
            <a data-role="button" data-rel="close">Close</a>
        </p>

    </div>

    <div data-role="header">
        <h1>Test Panel</h1>
    </div>

    <div role="main" class="ui-content">

        <a href="#leftPanel" data-role="button">Open My Panel!</a>
        <a href="#rightPanel" data-role="button">Open Another
Panel!</a>

    </div>


    <div data-role="panel" data-position="right" id="rightPanel">
        This is the right panel.

        <p>
            <a data-role="button" data-rel="close">Close</a>
        </p>

    </div>

</div>
```

In this example, two panels are defined, one above and one below the content div. Note that both have an ID. This is required so that the panel can be opened. Opening panels is done with a simple link. Inside the content div are two links—one for the left panel and one for the right panel. Panels are placed on the left-hand side by default. To place one on the right-hand side, add the data-position attribute. The final aspect to this is how panels are closed. By default, a panel will close if the user clicks anywhere *outside* the panel. Panels will also close if the user swipes. But since a user may not know this, it makes sense to also provide a manual way to close the panel. In both the panels, a link with a data-rel value of close is provided. Here's an example with the left panel opened:

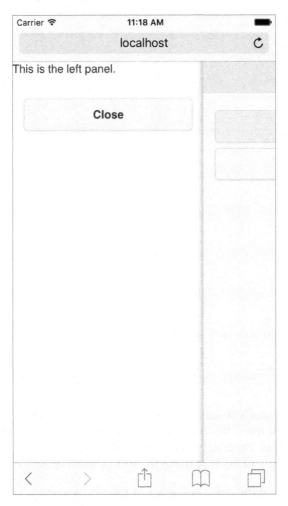

Notice that the `main` page content was pushed to the right. Panels are displayed in one of three ways and can be customized via the `data-display` attribute. The default value is `reveal`, and it pushes the content away. Another option is `overlay`. As you can guess, this will render the panel on top of the `main` page content.

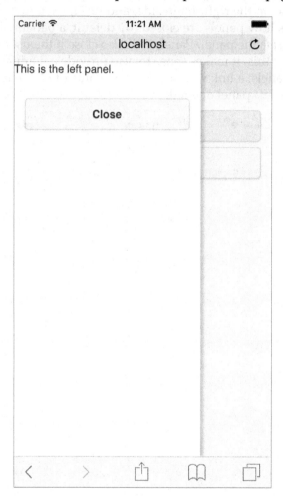

The final option is `push`. Push and reveal look very similar, and frankly, many users may not be able to tell the difference. Reveal will move the `main` page content to the side, *revealing* the panel. Push acts as if the panel is *pushing* the content to the side. You can see an example of both of these in `test_panel_display.html`.

Finally, you can control the close behavior of panels by using `data-swipe-close="false"` and `data-dismissible="false"`. The former disables the swipe that closes the behavior and the latter prevents the panel from closing by clicking outside the panel.

Using filterable widgets

The next widget we'll look at is the filterable widget. This is a generic concept of a widget that provides a way to automatically filter the data inside it. Imagine a large list. By allowing the user to filter, they can quickly focus on the content they are trying to find.

The general process for creating filterable content involves a few steps. You can begin by adding a `form` field that lets the user enter text. In theory, any content that throws a `change` event can be used, but in most cases, you'll want to use a simple text field. Next, you need to add `data-filter="true"` to the parent element whose children will be filtered. In the same element, you also need to provide `data-input` with a value that points to the jQuery selector of the text field you set up first. In general, this is the process. Let's consider a simple example:

```
Listing 7-9: test_filter.html
<div role="main" class="ui-content">

    <form>
    <input type="text" id="myFilter"
placeholder="Type to filter.">
    </form>

    <ul data-role="listview" data-filter="true"
data-input="#myFilter" data-inset="true">
            <li>Apples</li>
            <li>Bananas</li>
            <li>Cherries</li>
            <li>Donuts</li>
            <li>Eagles</li>
            <li>Foxes</li>
            <li>George</li>
            <li>Harry</li>
            <li>Ingrid</li>
            <li>Joker</li>
            <li>Kettle</li>
    </ul>

</div>
```

As you can see, we've got an input field on top (technically, it could be anywhere) and then a list beneath it. The list enables filtering and points to the ID of the input field. By default, the entire list is shown, but as the user types, the content is filtered:

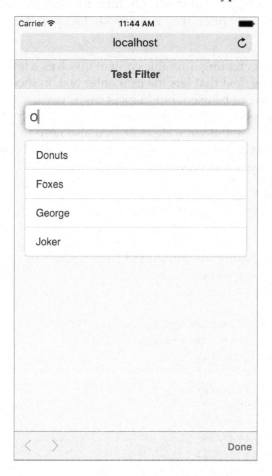

Filterable widgets also have a reversed mode called `reveal`. By adding `data-filter-reveal="true"` to the filtered widget, the content will be hidden and only show up as the user types content. Since this is an incredibly small change, we won't show the code for this, but you can play with an example in the file `test_filter_reveal.html`.

Finally, you can also customize how *matches* are made when filtering. If a child element contains a `data-filtertext` attribute, that value will be used to determine whether something is shown or hidden. You can also fully customize the matching logic with JavaScript for finer control.

Working with tabs

A recent addition to jQuery Mobile is actually a feature of a sister project, jQuery UI (http://www.jqueryui.com). The *tabs* widget follows the same format and usage as it does in jQuery UI, so we'll focus on the differences of the widget in jQuery Mobile.

Tabs consist of a list of tabs that serve as the labels for each particular tabbed display. For each tab panel, a `div` is created to host the content. The code in `Listing 7-10` shows an initial example:

```
Listing 7-10: tabs.html
<div role="main" class="ui-content">

    <div data-role="tabs">
        <ul>
                <li><a href="#tab1">Tab 1</a></li>
                <li><a href="#tab2">Tab 2</a></li>
                <li><a href="#tab3">Tab 3</a></li>
        </ul>

        <div id="tab1">
                <p>
                This is the first tab.
                </p>
        </div>

        <div id="tab2">
                <p>
                This is the second tab.
                </p>
        </div>

        <div id="tab3">
                <p>
                This is the third tab.
                </p>
        </div>

    </div>
```

As already stated, the list serves as a *navigation* for the tabs. jQuery Mobile (and jQuery UI) handles hiding and showing tab content based on what is clicked. Here is how the page is rendered:

As you can see, even though three different panels of div blocks exist, only the first one is shown. Clicking on any of the other links will load the appropriate panel. We can make this a lot prettier by switching from a simple list to navbar:

```
<div data-role="navbar">
<ul>
    <li><a href="#tab1">Tab 1</a></li>
    <li><a href="#tab2">Tab 2</a></li>
    <li><a href="#tab3">Tab 3</a></li>
</ul>
</div>
```

This renders as follows:

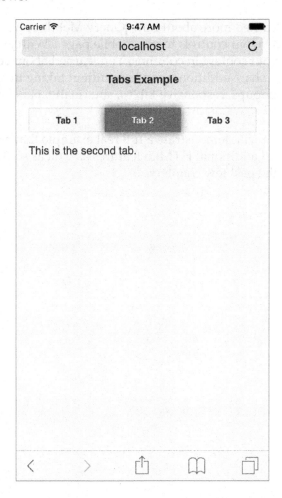

You can find an example of this in the file `tabs_better.html`.

Summary

In this chapter, you learned more about how jQuery Mobile enhances basic HTML to provide additional layout controls to our mobile pages. With grids, you learned a new way to easily layout content in columns. You learned about collapsible content blocks—a cool way to share additional content without taking up as much screen space. We looked at popups, responsive tables, and finally, panel controls and filterable content.

In the next chapter, we will demonstrate a full real example that creates a basic note tracker. It makes use of additional HTML5 features as well as some of the UI tips you've learned over the past few chapters.

8
Moving Further with the Notekeeper Mobile Application

In this chapter, we're going to begin assembling everything we've learned about lists, forms, pages, and content formatting into a suitable "mobile application", the Notekeeper application.

In this chapter, we will cover the following topics:

- Accepting user input using forms
- Storing user-inputted data locally using the HTML5 `localStorage` functionality
- How to add, edit, and remove items from the page dynamically

What is a mobile application?

Before writing our first mobile application, perhaps we should define what one is. Wikipedia says that a mobile application is a software application designed to run on smartphones, tablets, computers, and other mobile devices (`http://en.wikipedia.org/wiki/Mobile_app`). While it's true that jQuery Mobile apps are written in HTML, CSS, and JavaScript, this doesn't prevent them from being sophisticated pieces of software. They can certainly be developed with mobile devices in mind.

Some critics might note that it can't really be software unless it's *installed*. As you'll see later in the book, jQuery Mobile applications can actually be installed on a wide array of devices (including iOS, Android, and Windows Mobile) when coupled with the open source library, Cordova (`http://cordova.apache.org/`). This means that you'll be able to have your cake and eat it too. You might be asking yourself if the code written using jQuery Mobile can be considered as software, and as you'll find out in this chapter, the answer is yes.

Designing your first mobile application

The goal of any piece of software is to meet a need. Gmail met a need by freeing users from a single computer and letting them check their e-mail from any web browser. Photoshop met a need by allowing users to manipulate photos in ways no one had ever done. Our Notekeeper application will meet a need by allowing us to record simple notes for later reference. I know, it is sort of a letdown in comparison, but we've got to start somewhere right?

When building software, it's a good idea to spend time upfront writing out a specification for your project: what it will do, what it will look like, and what it should have.

Remember that if you don't know what you're building, how will you ever know whether it's done?

Listing out the requirements

We already know what we want our application to do: take notes. The problem is that there are so many ways that you could build a note-taking app that it's essential to sketch out just what we want ours to do. Not too much, not too little, but just enough for now. It's a point of fact with developers that our applications are never *done*, they're only finished *for now*. With Notekeeper, we've decided that we want to be able to do the following things with our application:

1. Adding a note.
2. Displaying a list of notes.
3. Viewing a note or deleting a note.

After deciding what tasks our app needs to accomplish, we need to decide how it will accomplish them. The easiest approach is to simply list those things down. By breaking each part down into smaller pieces, we make it easier to understand and to see just what we need to make it work. It's just like getting directions to your favorite restaurant; a left turn here, a roundabout there, and you're sitting down at the table before you know it. Let's look at each thing we want Notekeeper to do with the pieces and parts underneath:

1. Adding new notes (form).
2. A form container. All the user input widgets should be wrapped and contained within a form.
3. A title, the name of the note. This will also be used to display existing notes.
4. The note itself. The content or the body of the note.
5. A submit button. This will trigger the saving of the note.
6. Displaying a list of existing notes (`listview`).
7. A row item containing the title of the note. This row should be a link to a page containing the body of the note.
8. A section header row might be nice.
9. View note details (labels, paragraphs, or buttons).
10. A label for the title of the note.
11. A paragraph containing the content of the note.
12. A button labeled **Delete**.
13. A **Back** button.

Building your wireframes

Now that we've listed out the functionality for our app, how about we sketch each piece so that we get an idea of what we want it to look like? Don't worry if you failed art or if you can't draw a stick figure. Use a ruler if you have to or consider using Microsoft Excel or PowerPoint if you have these. You just need to be able to draw some boxes and some text labels. There are a number of free or inexpensive tools you can use for this purpose.

 A popular wireframing tool that runs in the browser is Balsamiq Mockups (`http://balsamiq.com/`).

Designing the Add Note wireframe

Now, what about the **Add Note** part? We decided that it needs a title, a box for the note, and a submit button. The form is an invisible container, so we don't need to draw it:

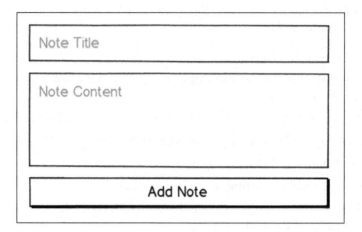

The Display Notes wireframe

The listview is an integral part of mobile development. It's the simplest way to group similar items together, plus it offers lots of extra functionality, such as scrolling and built-in images for links. We'll be using a listview to display our list of notes:

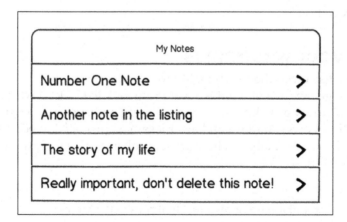

The View Note/Delete button wireframe

Finally, once we've added a note, we need to be able to delete the evidence; I mean clear out old notes to make way for new ones. Note that we've also sketched out a **Back** button. Once you start seeing things laid out, you'll find that you've forgotten something really important (like being able to return to the previous page), as shown in the following figure:

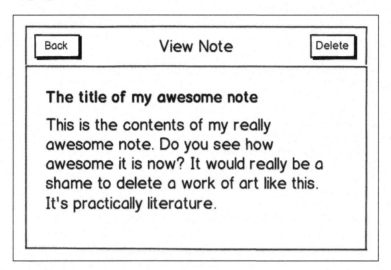

Writing the HTML

Now that our wireframes are done and we're happy with them, it's time to turn pencil drawings into ones and zeros. Since our app is relatively simple, none of the HTML should be difficult. You're more than halfway through the book after all and you should be doing these things in your sleep.

The HTML that you come up with should look remarkably like what's shown in the following code snippet. Let's examine it together:

```
Listing 8-1: notekeeper.html
<!DOCTYPE html>
<html>
<head>
<title>Notekeeper</title>
<meta name="viewport"
```

```
        content="width=device-width, initial-scale=1">
<link rel="stylesheet"
        href="http://code.jquery.com/mobile/1.4.5/jquery.mobile-
1.4.5.min.css" />
<script type="text/javascript"
        src="http://code.jquery.com/jquery-2.1.3.min.js">
</script>
<script type="text/javascript"
        src="http://code.jquery.com/mobile/1.4.5/jquery.mobile-
1.4.5.min.js">
</script>
<script src="js/application.js"></script>
</head>
<body>

   <div data-role="page">
        <div data-role="header">
             <h1>Notekeeper</h1>
        </div>

        <div role="main" class="ui-content">
        <form>
             <div class="ui-field-contain">
                  <input id="title" type="text" placeholder="Add a
note" />
             </div>
             <div class="ui-field-contain">
                  <textarea id="note" placeholder="The content of
your note">
                  </textarea>
             </div>
             <div class="ui-grid-a">
                  <div class="ui-block-a">
                       <input id="btnNoThanks" type="submit"
value="No Thanks" />
                  </div>
                  <div class="ui-block-b">
                       <input id="btnAddNote" type="button"
value="Add Note" />
                  </div>
             </div>
        </form>
```

```
              <ul id="notesList" data-role="listview" data-inset="true"></
ul>
   </div>

   <div data-role="footer" class="footer-docs">
          <h5>Intro to jQuery Mobile</h5>
   </div>
   </div>


</body>
</html>
```

Our Notekeeper application will make use of a single HTML file (notekeeper.
html) and a single JavaScript file (application.js). Up until this point, none of
the code you've written has really needed JavaScript. But once you begin writing
more complex applications, JavaScript will be a necessity. Preview the HTML from
Listing 8-1 in your web browser and you should see something similar to the
following screenshot:

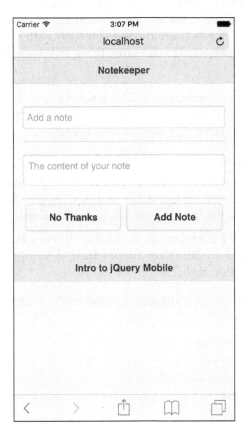

Notice that we're displaying the **Add Note** form on the same page as the view notes. With mobile application development, it's a good idea to condense things where possible. Don't make this a hard-and-fast rule, but since there's so little to our app, it's an acceptable decision to place both the parts together as long as they're clearly labeled. You can see that this page meets all the requirements we set for adding a note and for displaying our existing notes. It has a title input field, a note input field, and a **Save** button, and the entire thing is wrapped inside a `form` container. It also has `listview` that will be used to display our notes once we start adding them. What isn't seen here is a **Delete** button, but it will show up once we add our first note and view the **Details** page.

Adding functionality with JavaScript

As it is mentioned in this book, you don't need to write any JavaScript to get your money's worth from jQuery Mobile. But as you begin progressing in your experience with jQuery Mobile, you'll begin seeing how much additional value JavaScript can add to your projects. Before we look at the code, let's talk about how it will be structured. If you've done any web designing or development at all, you've probably seen JavaScript. It has been around since 1995 after all. The problem is that there are many different ways to do the same thing in JavaScript and not all of them are good.

The JavaScript code in this application will use what's called a design pattern. It's just a fancy term that specifies a certain structure for the code. There are three main reasons for using an existing design pattern are as follows:

1. It helps our code stay organized and tidy.

2. It prevents the variables and functions we write from being accidentally overwritten or altered by any other code we might add. A jQuery plugin perhaps or a code that's being loaded in from a third-party website.

3. It will help future developers to acclimatize themselves to your code much more rapidly. You are thinking about future developers as you work on the next Facebook killer, right?

Let's take a look at a very simple implementation of this design pattern before we jump into the full code:

```
Listing 8-2: kittyDressUp.js
$(document).ready(function(){
    // define the application name
    var kittyDressUp = {};
    (function(app){
```

```
        // set a few variables which can be used within the app
        var appName = 'Kitty Dress Up',
            version = '1.0';
        app.init = function(){
            // init is the typical name that developers give for the
            // code that runs when an application first loads
            // use whichever word you prefer
            var colors = app.colors();
        };
        app.colors = function(){
            var colors = ['red','blue','yellow','purple'];
            return colors;
        };
        app.init();
    })(kittyDressUp);
});
```

If you're familiar with JavaScript or jQuery, you'll probably see some elements that you recognize. For those readers who aren't familiar with jQuery or JavaScript, we'll review this example line by line. The `KittyDressUp.js` line starts off with jQuery's most recognizable element, `$(document).ready()`. Any code contained within this block waits to execute until the document, or the HTML page, is completely loaded. This means that you, the developer, can be assured that everything needed on the page is there before your code runs:

```
$(document).ready({
   // I'm ready captain!
});
```

In simple terms, the next line creates a variable named `kittyDressUp` and assigns it a value of an empty object. However, in our code, this new object will contain our entire application:

```
// define the application name
var kittyDressUp = {};
```

The following declaration is the core of the Kitty Dress Up application. It creates a function that accepts a single argument, and then immediately calls itself, passing in the empty object we created in the previous line. This concept is known as a **self-executing function** and is what keeps the external code from interfering with our application:

```
(function(app){
   // define the app functionality
})(kittyDressUp);
```

The next two lines set a few variables that can only be accessed from within the context or scope of our application:

```
// set a few variables which can be used within the app
var appName = 'Kitty Dress Up',
    version = '1.0';
```

Finally, the last few lines set up two functions that are available for use within the application. You can see that each function is assigned a name that is within the scope of the larger application. This is known as a **namespace**. The app variable is where the function lives, and the word after the dot (.) is the function name. Notice that within the init function, we're calling another function contained within the same application, app.colors(). We could reference any of the variables that we defined at the top as well:

```
app.init = function(){
    // init is the typical name that developers give for the
    // code that runs when an application first loads
    // use whatever word you prefer
    var colors = app.colors();
}
app.colors = function(){
    var colors = ['red','blue','yellow','purple'];
    return colors;
}
app.init();
```

Remember that app was the name of the parameter passed into the self-executing function and that its value is an empty object. Taken as a whole, these few lines create an object named kittyDressUp that contains two variables (appName and version), and two functions (init and colors). This example and the code for Notekeeper are simple examples, but they illustrate how to go about wrapping up code for various pieces of a larger app into discrete packages. In fact, after kittyDressUp.js runs, you could even pass kittyDressUp into yet another set of code for use there.

Phew! Everyone take five. You've earned it.

Storing Notekeeper data

Now that we're back from our 5 minutes break, it's time to roll up our sleeves and get to work, adding functionality to our app. While we've talked about how we want Notekeeper to behave, we haven't discussed the core issue of where to store the note data. There are a few possibilities, all of which have pros and cons. Let's list them out:

- **Database (MySQL, SQL Server, and PostgreSQL)**: While a database would be the ideal solution, it's a little complex for our app. It requires Internet connectivity, and you'd need a server-side component (ColdFusion, PHP, or .NET) acting as a middle man to save notes to the database.

- **Text file**: Text files are great because they take up very little room. The problem is that as a web app, Notekeeper can't save files to the user's device.

- **localStorage**: This stores information in the user's machine in key/value pairs. It's got a size limit, but it's pretty large for plain text. Most modern browsers support it, and it can be used in the offline mode.

Using localStorage

For the purposes of this chapter, we'll be selecting `localStorage` as our method of choice. Let's take a quick look at how it behaves so that you'll be familiar with it when you see it. As mentioned previously, `localStorage` works on the premise of storing data in key/value pairs. Saving a value to `localStorage` works in one of the two ways and is easy no matter which one you choose:

```
localStorage.setItem('keyname','this is the value I am saving');
```

Alternatively you can use this as well:

```
localStorage['keyname'] = 'this is the value I am saving';
```

Which version you choose is a personal preference, but because it involves slightly less typing, we'll be using the second method, square brackets. One issue we'll run into is that `localStorage` can't directly store complex data, such as arrays or objects. It only stores strings. That's a problem because we're going to be storing all of our data inside one variable so that we always know where it lives. Never fear, we can pull a fast one on `localStorage` and convert our complex object into a string representation of itself using a built-in function called `stringify()`. This conversion process, from a complex object to a string, is called **serialization**.

The following code snippet shows how it works:

```
// create our notes object
var notes = {
   'note number one': 'this is the contents of note number one', 'make
     conference call': 'call Evan today'
   }
// convert it to a string, then store it.
localStorage['Notekeeper'] = JSON.stringify(Notekeeper);
```

Retrieving a value is just as simple as setting it; it also offers two options. You'll usually want to define a variable to receive the contents of the `localStorage` variable. You can do so using the following line of code:

```
var family = localStorage.getItem('my family');
```

Alternatively, you can use this:

```
var family = localStorage['my family'];
```

If you're retrieving a complex value, you need to perform an additional step before you can use the contents of the variable. As we just mentioned, to store complex values, you must first use the `stringify()` function, which has a counterpart function called `parse()`. The `parse()` function takes the string containing that complex object and turns it back into pure JavaScript (a process called **deserialization**). It's used as follows:

```
var myFamily = ['andy', 'jaime', 'noelle', 'evan', 'mason', 'henry'];
localStorage['family'] = JSON.stringify(myFamily);
var getFamily = JSON.parse(localStorage['family']);
```

Finally, if ever you wanted to delete the key completely, then you can accomplish it in a single line of code, again with two flavors:

```
localStorage.removeItem('family');
```

Or, you could use the following line of code:

```
delete localStorage['family'];
```

It's worth noting that if you try to retrieve a key that doesn't exist within `localStorage`, JavaScript won't throw an error. It'll just return `undefined`, which is JavaScript's way of saying sorry, but there is nothing. The following code snippet is an example:

```
var missing = localStorage['yertl the turtle'];
console.log(missing);
// returns undefined
```

Effective use of boilerplates

There's one last thing left before we start building our JavaScript file. In our application, we're only going to have one JavaScript file, and it's going to contain the entire codebase. This is fine for smaller apps like ours, but it's a bad idea for larger apps. It's better to break up your project into distinct pieces and then put each of them into their own files. This makes it easier for the teams of developers to work together (for example, Evan works on the login process, while Henry builds the list of vendors). It also makes each file smaller and easier to understand because it only addresses one part of the whole. If you want all of the pieces of your app to have a similar structure and design, it's a good idea to start each section with a boilerplate. We'll be using a boilerplate for our app's only file (that you can see in the following code snippet, `Listing 8-3`). You might notice that it looks very similar to the `kittyDressUp` example, and you'd be right:

```
Listing 8-3: application.js
$(function(){
  // define the application
  var Notekeeper = {};
  (function(app){
    // variable definitions go here
    app.init = function(){
      // stuff in here runs first
    }
    app.init();
  })(Notekeeper);
});
```

Building the Add Note feature

At last, we can start building! Since it's difficult to display a list of notes that don't exist, much less delete one, we'll start writing the **Add Note** functionality first. For users to be able to add a note, they have to enter a title and the contents of a note and then hit the submit button. So, let's start here.

Adding bindings

We're going to create a new empty function block under the `app.init()` function's definition. It should look something like the following line of code:

```
app.bindings = function(){
}
```

The `bindings` function will contain any piece of code that needs to be fired when a user does something in our app, such as clicking on the submit button or the **Delete** button. We group this code together for the sake of organization. Within the `bindings()` function, we're going to add the following lines. This will fire when a user clicks on the submit button on the **Add Note** form:

```
// set up binding for form
$('#btnAddNote').on('touchend', function(e){
  e.preventDefault();
  // save the note
  app.addNote(
    $('#title').val(),
    $('#note').val()
  );
});
```

jQuery's `val()` function is a shorthand method used to get the current value of any form input field.

The following points are a few notes about this new addition:

- When using jQuery, there will always be more than one way to accomplish something. In most cases, you will simply pick the one that you like the best (they usually offer an identical performance).

- Notice that the `.on()` method accepts a single parameter, `e`, which is the event object (in this case, a click event). We call `e.preventDefault()` to stop the standard touch event from happening on this element, but we still allow the remaining code to continue running. You might have seen other developers use `return false`, but jQuery's best practices recommend using `e.preventDefault()` instead.

- Within the `touchend` binding, we're calling the `addNote` function and passing into it the title typed in by the user and the note. The whitespace is unimportant, serving merely to make it easier to see what we're doing.

Even though we've added the binding to our code, if you run the app right now, nothing will happen when you click on the **Add Note** button. The reason is that nothing has actually called the `bindings()` function yet. Add the following line inside the `init()` function and you'll be ready to go:

```
app.init = function(){
  app.bindings();
}
```

Collecting and storing data

Next, we will add another new empty function block under `app.bindings`:

```
app.addNote = function(title, note){
}
```

Now, because we're storing all of our notes into one key within `localStorage`, we first need to check to see whether any notes already exist. Retrieve the `Notekeeper` key from `localStorage`, save it to a variable, and then compare it. If the value of the key we ask for is an empty string or `undefined`, we'll need to create an empty object. If there is a value, then we will take it and use the `parse()` function to turn it into JavaScript:

```
var notes = localStorage['Notekeeper'];
if (notes == undefined || notes == '') {
  var notesObj = {};
} else {
  var notesObj = JSON.parse(notes)
}
```

Notice that we're expecting two variables to be passed into the `addNote()` function: `title` and `note`. Next, we will replace any spaces in the title with dashes. This makes it easier for some browsers to understand the string of text. Then, we will place the key/value pair into our newly minted notes object:

```
notesObj[title.replace(/ /g,'-')] = note;
```

The JavaScript `replace` method makes string manipulation quite simple. It acts on a string, taking a search term and a replacement term. The search term can be a simple string or a complex regular expression.

The next step is to take our `notesObj` variable, apply the `stringify()` function to it, and place it into `localStorage`. We then clear the values from the two input fields to make it easier for the user to input another note. As a rule in building software, it's a nice touch to return the interface to its original state after an action, such as adding or removing content:

```
localStorage['Notekeeper'] = JSON.stringify(notesObj);
// clear the two form fields
$note.val('');
$title.val('');
//update the listview
app.displayNotes();
```

All of these variable definitions should be familiar to you with perhaps one exception that we should point out. Many jQuery developers like to use conventional naming for variables that contain jQuery objects. Specifically, they prepend the variable name with a $ sign just like with jQuery. This lets them or future developers know what's contained within the variable. Let's go ahead and add these definitions to the top of our app. Just after the line that reads `// variable definitions go here`, add the following lines. They refer to the `title` input field and the note `textarea` field, respectively:

```
var $title = $('#title'),
    $note = $('#note');
```

As a final step to this function, we will fire off a call to `app.displayNotes()` to update the list of notes. Since this function doesn't exist yet, let's create it next.

Building the Display Notes feature

You probably tested out the **Add Note** feature while writing the previous section. This means that you'll have at least one note saved in `localStorage` for use while testing the **Display Notes** feature. By now, you're familiar with our first step for any new section. Go ahead and add your empty `displayNotes()` function to hold our code:

```
app.displayNotes = function(){
}
```

Next, we need to retrieve all of our notes from `localStorage`:

```
// get notes
var notes = localStorage['Notekeeper'];
// convert notes from string to object
return JSON.parse(notes);
```

You might start seeing a pattern with many of our functions. Almost all of them begin with us retrieving notes from `localStorage`. While there are only two lines of code needed to perform this task, there's no need for us to repeat those two lines each time we need to get the notes. So, we're going to write a quick helper function containing those two lines. It looks similar to the following code snippet:

```
app.getNotes = function(){
  // get notes
  var notes = localStorage['Notekeeper'];
  // convert notes from string to object
  if(notes) return JSON.parse(notes);
  return [];
}
```

With our new helper function in place, we can use it in the `displayNotes()` function, as shown in the following code snippet:

```
app.displayNotes = function(){
  // get notes
  var notesObj = app.getNotes();
}
```

Now that we have the `notesObj` variable containing our packet of notes, we need to loop over this packet and output the contents:

```
// create an empty string to contain html
var notesObj = app.getNotes(),
      html = '',
      n; // make sure your iterators are properly scoped
// loop over notes
for (n in notesObj) {
  html += li.replace(/ID/g,n.replace(/-/g, ' ')).replace(/LINK/g,n);
}
$ul.html(notesHdr + html).listview('refresh');
```

It might seem odd for the line inside the `for` loop to have multiple `replace` statements, but the nature of JavaScript allows for methods to be chained. Chaining allows us to run multiple operations (on the same element) within a single statement. Adding an additional method call simply repeats the process.

There might be some new concepts in this code block, so let's take a closer look. The variable named `html` is nothing special, but how we're using it might be. As we loop over the existing notes, we're storing new information into the `html` variable along with whatever else is there inside it. We accomplish this by using the `+=` operator that allows us to assign and append at the same time.

The second thing you might notice is `li` on the right-hand side of the assignment. Where does this come from? That's a template for a single list item that has not yet been created. Let's create it before we talk about it. At the top of your `app.js` file, just after the line that reads `// variable definitions go here`, add the following lines of code:

```
var $title = $('#title'),
    $note = $('#note'),
    $ul = $('#notesList'),
    li = '<li><a href="#pgNotesDetail?title=LINK">ID</a></li>',
```

You're already familiar with the convention of adding $ before a variable to indicate a jQuery object. That's what we're doing with the `$ul` variable. The second new variable, `li`, is slightly different. This contains the HTML for a single list item that will display a notes title. The best practice is to avoid mixing HTML or CSS in with your JavaScript wherever possible. We're declaring this as a template now in case we decide to use it in multiple places later.

The other part that might be of interest is the way we're using the `li` variable. When calling the string `replace` function, we're looking for all the occurrences of the word LINK (uppercase intended) and replacing it with the title of the note. Because JavaScript is a case-sensitive language, it's a safe assumption that we won't be running into a natural occurrence of that word.

Dynamically adding notes to our listview

There's one final thing we need to put in place before our notes show up on the page. You might have noticed that the only place that calls the `displayNotes()` function appears within the `addNote()` function. This is a good place for it, but it can't be the only place. We need something that runs when the page first loads. The prime place for this would be in the `init()` function, and this is where we'll place it.

There's one problem though; we can't just load our notes and run. What will happen if there are no notes? We need a nice message to display to the user so that they don't think something's wrong. Let's create a new function called `app.checkForStorage()` that handles all of this:

```
app.checkForStorage = function(){
    var notes = app.getNotes();
    // are there existing notes?
    if (!$.isEmptyObject(notes)) {
        // yes there are. pass them off to be displayed
        app.displayNotes();
    } else {
        // nope, just show the placeholder
        $ul.html(notesHdr + noNotes).listview('refresh');
    }
};
```

By now, all of this should be familiar to you: calling our `app.getNotes()` method for notes and calling the `displayNotes()` function if it finds them. The second part has some new items though. When we set the HTML for the `$ul` jQuery object, we're calling two new variables—one for the `listview` header and another if we don't have any notes.

Let's add those two variable definitions now. Under // `variable definitions go here`, add the following two lines:

```
var $title = $('#title'),
    $note = $('#note'),
    $ul = $('#notesList'),
    li = '<li><a href="#pgNotesDetail?title=LINK">ID</a></li>'
    notesHdr = '<li data-role="list-divider">Your Notes</li>',
    noNotes = '<li id="noNotes">You have no notes</li>';
```

The last part of the line might normally go unnoticed, but we won't let it. It's really crucial. jQuery Mobile offers developers with options: the option of having static HTML code that's already on the page when it loads. jQuery Mobile also provides an option for adding HTML code on the fly. This really gives developers a lot of flexibility, but it presents a unique challenge as well. By design, jQuery Mobile converts HTML into stylish-looking widgets before displaying the page to the user. This means that any HTML added after that will be presented to the user without any style.

However, jQuery Mobile also offers a way to get around this by building in the ability to refresh each and every element that it converts. Most of them have a built-in function corresponding to the name of the element; in our case, it's the `listview()` function. Actually, this method offers the ability to add a completely new `listview` to the page. In our situation, we only care about refreshing the one we have, so we will simply add the `refresh` keyword and jQuery Mobile will convert your plain text in `listview`. Try leaving that last part off and see just how much work jQuery Mobile saves you. Maybe, you should add the jQuery Mobile team to your Christmas card list?

Finally, we have to actually call our newest function. Within the `init()` function, add the following line. Then, reload the page and watch your notes load:

```
app.checkForStorage();
```

Viewing a note

At this point, we should be able to create a new note and have that note be immediately displayed in our `listview`. In fact, the rows in `listview` are already links; they just don't work. Let's change that right now.

Using the .on() method

Add the following lines to the `bindings()` function:

```
$(document).on('touchend', '#notesList a', function(e){
    e.preventDefault();
    var href = $(this)[0].href.match(/\?.*$/)[0];
    var title = href.replace(/^\?title=/,'');
    app.loadNote(title);
});
```

This new binding has a few new concepts, so let's unpack them. First up, we're not using the `bind` function. Instead, we are using jQuery's `on()` function. The difference is that `bind()` only works on existing page elements, whereas `on()` is proactive. It works on existing elements as well as on the ones that get created after the binding is applied.

The second and third lines of the binding might look a little confusing, but they only do one thing. They retrieve the URL from the `href` attribute of the link that was clicked. The `li` template we defined earlier in the chapter contains the following URL for each list item:

```
#pgNotesDetail?title=LINK
```

After the `displayNote()` function runs, the URL will look as follows (run your mouse over each list item to see the link displayed at the bottom of your browser window):

```
#pgNotesDetail?title=the-title-of-the-note
```

Finally, we will tell our code to run a new function appropriately named `app.loadNote()`.

Dynamically creating a new page

If you haven't already created the new empty function block for your new `loadNote()` function, go ahead and do it now. Remember that we're passing in the title of the note we want to view, so make sure to add that as an argument in the `loadNote()` function:

```
app.loadNote = function(title){
}
```

Then, place the following lines at the top of the function:

```
// get notes
var notes = app.getNotes(),
      // lookup specific note
      note = notes[title],
      // define the "new page" template
      page = ['<div data-role="page" data-url="details">',
            '<div data-role="header" data-add-back-btn="true">',
               '<h1>Notekeeper</h1>',
               '<a id="btnDelete" href="" data-href="ID" data-
role="button" class="ui-btn-right">Delete</a>',
            '</div>',
            '<div role="main" class="ui-content"><h3>TITLE</
h3><p>NOTE</p></div>',
         '</div>'].join(''),
```

The first line retrieves our note object, while the second line pulls the specific note that the user has requested. The third variable's definition breaks the rule we mentioned earlier in the chapter about mixing HTML and JavaScript, but every rule has exceptions. We're defining it here as opposed to the header of our .js file, since this is the only place it is needed. This still serves the purpose of keeping the document organized.

The page variable now contains all of the HTML needed to display a note details page to the user. Do you recall that our app has only one HTML file? We're actually creating an entire page from scratch using the previous HTML code. There are also some details in it worth pointing out. They are as follows:

- By default, jQuery Mobile does not offer a Back button for pages. You can, however, enable one on a page-by-page basis using the data-add-back-btn="true" attribute on any div tag that also has a data-role="header" attribute.

- The data-url attribute is an identifier used by jQuery Mobile so that it can keep track of the multiple pages that are generated.

- This approach to string concatenation might look different to you. When you only have a few words, it's okay to say andy + jaime, but when you have multiple lines, a nice trick is to create an array where each line is an item in the array. Then you join each item together and presto! It has the added benefit of keeping things neat and tidy too.

Now that we have a whole page contained within a variable, what can we do with it? The first thing we can do is to turn it into a jQuery object. By wrapping any distinct chunk of HTML with `$()`, you can turn it into a Grade-A jQuery object:

```
newPage = $(page);
```

Then, you can take the HTML of that newly created page and replace parts of it with the values from your selected note:

```
// append it to the page container
newPage.html(function(index, old){
  return old
    .replace(/ID/g,title)
    .replace(/TITLE/g,title)
    .replace(/-/g,' '))
    .replace(/NOTE/g,note)
}).appendTo($.mobile.pageContainer);
```

Since Version 1.4, jQuery has offered the option of **callback** within certain functions. These include `.html()`, `.text()`, `.css()`, and a few others. This function expects two arguments, of which the second contains the full HTML currently contained within the matching element. This means that we can make tweaks to the HTML contained inside our `newPage` variable without having to completely change it. Wonderful isn't it?

Next, we're appending the entire `newPage` variable to the end of the current page referenced here by the `$.mobile.pageContainer` constant. Finally, because we cancelled the default click action in our binding, we have to tell the link to perform an action, that is, to forward the user to this newly created page. jQuery Mobile offers a built-in way to do this:

```
$.mobile.changePage(newPage);
```

Now for the grand revelation. If you load up `notekeeper.html` in your browser, you should be able to add, display, and finally view notes, all within the confines of a single browser window:

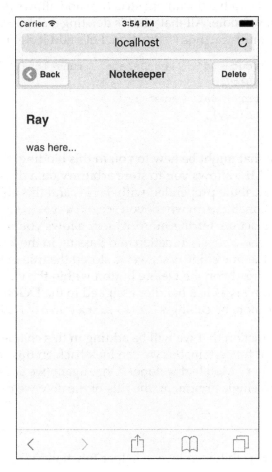

Isn't jQuery Mobile great?

Deleting a note

Looking back to the requirements for our app, we're doing pretty well. We've written an HTML code that sets up the document structure and allows us to add a note, display notes, and view a note. All that's left is deleting a note, and it begins with a last binding set up in our `bindings()` function. Let's add it right now:

```
$(document).on('touchend', '#btnDelete', function(e){
    e.preventDefault();
    var key = $(this).data('href');
    app.deleteNote(key);
});
```

There's only one item that might be new to you in this binding, the use of jQuery's `.data()` function. HTML5 allows you to store arbitrary data directly on any HTML element by using an attribute prepended with `data-`, and this ability is at the core of jQuery Mobile's functionality. Anywhere you see `data-role="something"`, you're seeing HTML5 data in action. Furthermore, jQuery allows you to retrieve any `data-` value by using the `.data()` function and passing in the key of the item you want to view. In the preceding case, we've stored the title of the note into a `data-href` attribute directly on the **Delete** button within the view page. Because the binding we're adding is a click handler assigned to the **Delete** button, we can retrieve the title of the note by calling `$(this).data('href')`. Neat-o!

This will be the last function that we will be adding in this chapter. Are you sad? It's a poignant moment for certain, but we can look back on this with fondness after you're a successful jQuery Mobile developer. Once again, we start with an empty function that accepts a single argument, the title of the note we're deleting:

```
app.deleteNote = function(key){
}
```

The function definition is followed by our helper function for retrieving notes:

```
// get the notes from localStorage
var notesObj = app.getNotes();
```

Then, we will delete the note. You've already seen this in action when we reviewed `localStorage`, so it should be familiar to you:

```
// delete selected note
delete notesObj[key];
// write it back to localStorage
localStorage['Notekeeper'] = JSON.stringify(notesObj);
```

Deleting the note is followed in quick succession by writing the remaining notes back to `localStorage`. The final two lines in the `deleteNote()` function take us back to the main page of the app, the list of notes. They also trigger the original `checkForStorage()` function:

```
// return to the list of notes
$.mobile.changePage('notekeeper.html');
// restart the storage check
app.checkForStorage();
```

The last line may seem odd to you, but keep in mind that we don't know in advance if there are still any notes left. Running through the storage check allows us to display the placeholder text in case there are no notes. It's a good habit to get into, as it helps our app become less prone to errors:

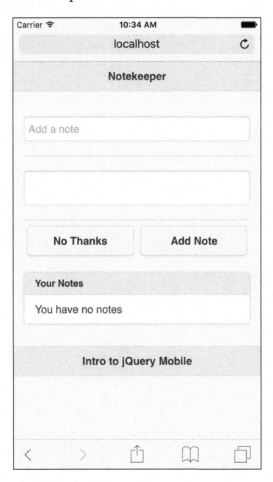

Summary

In this chapter, we built a living, breathing mobile application with jQuery Mobile. Stop and give yourself a pat on the back. We walked through the process of listing the requirements for our app, building the wireframes, and writing the HTML. You learned about HTML5's localStorage using the templates for text replacement, and some of the cooler features of jQuery Mobile, including dynamically adding and refreshing elements on the page.

In the next chapter, you'll learn how to set global configuration options for jQuery Mobile and how to use other utility APIs within jQuery Mobile to streamline your code and take advantage of the great work the jQuery Mobile team has already done on your behalf.

9
jQuery Mobile Configuration, Utilities, and JavaScript Methods

In this chapter, we will look at how JavaScript can be used to further configure and enhance jQuery Mobile websites. So far, we've made use of HTML and CSS to generate everything. Now, we'll look at additional scripting that adds additional functionality to your websites.

In this chapter, we will be covering the following topics:

- How jQuery Mobile websites can be configured via JavaScript
- The various JavaScript utilities that ship with jQuery Mobile and how they can be used
- The APIs used to work with the enhanced jQuery Mobile form and widget controls

Configuring jQuery Mobile

jQuery Mobile does many things for you—from improving page navigation to changing how form controls work. All of this is done in an effort to make your content work better in a mobile environment. There will be times, however, when you would not want jQuery Mobile to do something, or perhaps, you would simply want to slightly tweak how the framework acts. That's where configuration comes in.

To configure a jQuery Mobile website, you begin by writing a code that listens for the `mobileinit` event. This can be done using a normal jQuery event handler similar to the following code snippet:

```
$(document).bind("mobileinit", function() {
  //your customization here
});
```

For this event to be captured, you must configure it before jQuery Mobile is actually loaded. The simplest way to do this, and the way recommended by the jQuery Mobile documents, is simply placing this code in a script loaded before the jQuery Mobile JavaScript library. The following code snippet shows what the header of our files typically look like:

```
<!DOCTYPE html>
<html>
<head>
<title>Tabs Example</title>
<meta name="viewport"
content="width=device-width, initial-scale=1">
<link rel="stylesheet" href = "http://code.jquery.com/mobile/1.4.5/
jquery.mobile-1.4.5.min.css" />
<script type="text/javascript"
src="http://code.jquery.com/jquery-2.1.3.min.js">
</script>
<script type="text/javascript"  src = "http://code.jquery.com/
mobile/1.4.5/jquery.mobile-1.4.5.min.js">
</script>
</head>
```

Notice that the jQuery Mobile library is the last one loaded. We can simply add in a new `script` tag before it:

```
<!DOCTYPE html>
<html>
<head>
<title>Tabs Example</title>
<meta name="viewport"
content="width=device-width, initial-scale=1">
<link rel="stylesheet" href = "http://code.jquery.com/mobile/1.4.5/
jquery.mobile-1.4.5.min.css" />
<script type="text/javascript"
src="http://code.jquery.com/jquery-2.1.3.min.js">
</script>
<script src="config.js"></script>
```

```
<script type="text/javascript"  src = "http://code.jquery.com/
mobile/1.4.5/jquery.mobile-1.4.5.min.js">
</script>
</head>
```

Configuring jQuery Mobile is as simple as updating the `$.mobile` object.
The following code snippet is a simple example:

```
$(document).bind("mobileinit",  function() {
  $.mobile.someSetting="some value here";
});
```

This object contains a set of key/value pairs for the various settings that can be
configured. You don't actually create it—it exists when the event handler is run.
Another option is to make use of jQuery's `extend()` functionality, as shown in the
following code snippet:

```
$(document).bind("mobileinit",  function() {
  $.extend($.mobile, {
    someSetting:"some value here"
  });
});
```

Both forms are okay and they work absolutely the same. Use whichever feels more
comfortable. Now, let's look at the various configuration options:

Settings	Use
ns	This is the namespace value used for data attributes. It defaults to nothing. You will specify a value here if you want to prefix the jQuery Mobile-recognized data attributes. So, for example, if you wanted to use `data-jqm-role="page"` instead of `data-role="page"`, you would configure the ns value to be `jqm`.
ajaxEnabled	We discussed before how AJAX is used for both page loads and form submissions. If you wish to disable this, set this value to `false`. The default, obviously, is `true`.
allowCrossDomainPages	This is a security setting that defaults to `false`. Setting this to `true` allows for remote pages to be loaded via `$.mobile.loadPage`. This is normally required only for PhoneGap applications that load content from another server.

Settings	Use
`autoInitializePage`	Normally, jQuery Mobile will run `$.mobile.initializePage` on load. This displays the rendered page (at the moment, this particular function isn't properly documented). If you wish to disable this default value, set `autoInitializePage` to `false`. You will need to run `$.mobile.initializePage` manually.
`defaultPageTransition`	Like the previous option, this setting is used for transitions. This time, it is used for page loads. The default is `fade` and the options similar to the previous option are possible.
`dynamicBaseEnabled`	This is used to signal if a dynamic base tag is used. This defaults to `true` and should only be set to `false` if you're using another web framework that requires a particular base tag reference.
`degradeInputs`	This determines what the various form input types should be degraded into when a particular type is considered "`unsafe`". This setting is an object of keys with one key per input type. Currently, only `range` and `search` are modified (both to `text`).
`dynamicBaseEnabled`	Normally, jQuery Mobile will use a dynamic base attribute to help load resources. You can disable this by setting this value to `false`.
`gradeA`	This is used to determine what actually constitutes a *good* browser. This is handled by jQuery Mobile; but if you want to overrule the framework or define some other condition that must be met, you would provide a function here that returns a Boolean value (`true` or `false`).
`getMaxScrollForTransition`	One of the performance tricks jQuery Mobile uses is to automatically disable page transitions if you're navigating from or to a page that is *very* long. So, for example, imagine you're at the bottom of a very long page and you're clicking on a link to load a new page. If jQuery Mobile determines that you've scrolled to a value three times the window height, it will disable the transition. This value, 3, can be configured by this property.
`hashListeningEnabled`	This refers to the ability to listen to changes in the `location.hash` property of the browser. jQuery Mobile handles this normally; but if the value is set to `false`, you can write your own code to respond to these changes.

Settings	Use
ignoreContentEnabled	Normally, jQuery Mobile automatically enhances everything it can. You can disable this in some cases at a control level, but you can also tell jQuery Mobile to ignore everything within a particular container by adding data-enhance=true. If you make use of this feature, then your configuration must set ignoreContentEnabled to true. This tells jQuery Mobile to look for, and respect, that particular flag. This is set to false by default, and it allows jQuery Mobile to do its magic a bit faster.
keepNative	This is a selector value that will be used to prevent items from being enhanced.
linkBindingEnabled	jQuery Mobile typically listens to all the link clicks. If you wish to disable this globally, you can do so with this setting.
maxTransitionWidth	This is used to set the maximum size for transitions. If set to a value that is smaller than the window it will be transitioned *into*, then no visual transition will be used.
pageLoadErrorMessage	This is a message shown to users if an error occurs when loading a page. The default is **Error Loading Page**, but it can be changed for localization (or any reason).
pageLoadErrorMessageTheme	The theme to be used when a page load error dialog is displayed. The default is e.
phonegapNavigationEnabled	If enabled, PhoneGap's navigation helper will be used when sending the user to their previous location. This was added to help with issues under Android. The default is false.
pushStateEnabled	This tells jQuery Mobile to use the HTML5 pushState functionality instead of the hash-based changes for page navigation. This defaults to true.
transitionFallbacks	This is not a simple setting but rather a hashmap that allows you to specify a fallback for a transition that is not supported on a device. So, for example, you can specify that the fallback for the slide transition is pop by doing this: transitionFallbacks["slide"] = "pop".

That's quite a few options. But typically, you will only need to configure one or two of these settings. Let's look at a simple example where a few of these are put to use. The code in `Listing 9-1` is the home page for the application. Note the use of the additional `script` tag to load our configuration:

```
Listing 9-1: test1.html
<!DOCTYPE html>
<html>
<head>
<title>Page Transition Test</title>
<meta name="viewport"
      content="width=device-width, initial-scale=1">
<link rel="stylesheet"
      href="http://code.jquery.com/mobile/1.4.5/jquery.mobile-
1.4.5.min.css" />
<script type="text/javascript"
        src="http://code.jquery.com/jquery-2.1.3.min.js">
</script>
<script src="config.js"></script>
<script type="text/javascript"
        src="http://code.jquery.com/mobile/1.4.5/jquery.mobile-
1.4.5.min.js">
</script>
</head>

<body>

<div data-role="page" id="first">

    <div data-role="header">
        <h1>Dialog Test</h1>
    </div>

    <div role="main" class="ui-content">

        <p>
        <a href="#page2">Another Page</a><br/>
        <a href="test2.html">Yet Another Page</a><br/>
        </p>

    </div>

</div>
```

```
<div data-role="page" id="page2">

    <div data-role="header">
         <h1>The Second</h1>
    </div>

    <div role="main" class="ui-content">

         <p>
         This is the Second. Go <a href="#first">first</a>.
         </p>

    </div>

</div>

</body>
</html>
```

The file contains two jQuery Mobile pages and links to another in `test2.html`. That page simply provides a link back, so it will not be included in the text. Now let's look at `config.js`:

```
Listing 9-2: config.js
$(document).bind("mobileinit", function() {
   $.mobile.defaultPageTransition = "none";
});
```

In `config.js`, one setting is modified—the default page transition.

In an earlier chapter, we discussed forms and how jQuery Mobile automatically enhances controls. While you can suppress this enhancement on a control within your HTML, you can also tell jQuery Mobile a list of controls that it should never enhance. To set this list, specify a value for `$.mobile.keepNative`. The value should be a list of selectors. Any field that matches one of the selectors will *not* be enhanced (as a reminder, you can disable the form field autoenhancement in HTML by adding `data-role="none"` to your form field). The code in `Listing 9-3` demonstrates an example of this:

```
Listing 9-3: form.html
<!DOCTYPE html>
<html>
<head>
<title>Page Transition Test</title>
<meta name="viewport"
```

```
        content="width=device-width, initial-scale=1">
<link rel="stylesheet"
        href="http://code.jquery.com/mobile/1.4.5/jquery.mobile-
1.4.5.min.css" />
<script type="text/javascript"
        src="http://code.jquery.com/jquery-2.1.3.min.js">
</script>
<script src="config2.js"></script>
<script type="text/javascript"
        src="http://code.jquery.com/mobile/1.4.5/jquery.mobile-
1.4.5.min.js">
</script>
</head>

<body>

<div data-role="page" id="first">

    <div data-role="header">
        <h1>Form Test</h1>
    </div>

    <div role="main" class="ui-content">

        <div data-role="fieldcontain">
            <label for="name">Name:</label>
            <input type="text" name="name" id="name"
             value=""  />
        </div>

        <div data-role="fieldcontain">
            <label for="email">Email:</label>
            <input type="text" name="email" id="email"
             value="" class="boring"  />
        </div>

    </div>

</div>

</body>
</html>
```

Notice two things in particular. First, we're loading a configuration file in the header of the page. Second, our form has two text fields, but we've added a class to the second one, `boring`. The code in `Listing 9-4` is our configuration file:

```
Listing 9-4: config2.js
$(document).bind("mobileinit", function() {
    $.mobile.keepNative = "input.boring";
});
```

We've specified that we want input tags with the class of `boring` to *not* be enhanced. The result is as follows:

Using jQuery Mobile utilities

Now that we've covered jQuery Mobile configuration, let's take a look at the utilities available to your applications. These are utilities provided by the framework, and they can be used in any application. You may not need them all (or any) on your website, but knowing they are there can help save time in the future.

Page methods and utilities

Let's begin looking at methods and utilities related to pages and the navigation between them. jQuery Mobile uses the concept of a **page container** to reference not one page or the current page, but the place where all the pages are loaded dynamically. In the current version of jQuery Mobile, there is one page container at any time, but in the future, this may change. Let's look at these methods and utilities related to the page container:

- change(to, options): This method is used to change to another page. The first argument, to, can be either a string (the URL) or a jQuery DOM object. The options argument is an optional object of the key/value pairs. These options are as follows:

    ° allowSamePageTransition: Normally, jQuery Mobile will not allow you to transition to the same page. But if set to false, this will be allowed.

    ° changeHash: This determines whether the URL should change.

    ° data: This can be either a string or an object of the values passed to the next page.

    ° dataUrl: This value is used for the URL in the browser. This is normally set by the page the user is being sent to. You can override this here.

    ° loadMsgDelay: This value specifies when a loading message should be shown. If the new page loads *before* this time, the loading message won't be used. This defaults to 50.

    ° reload: Normally, jQuery Mobile will not reload a page that is already loaded. Setting this to true forces a reload.

    ° reverse: This determines the *direction* of the transition.

    ° role: jQuery Mobile will typically look for the data-role attribute of the page loaded. To specify another role, set this option.

    ° showLoadMsg: Normally, jQuery Mobile shows a loading message when a page is fetched. You can disable this by setting this value to false.

- ° transition: This is set to determine which transition you wish to use. Remember, this can be configured at a global level as well.

- ° type: We mentioned earlier that jQuery Mobile loads in new pages via an AJAX-based request. The type option allows you to specify the HTTP method used to load the page. The default is get.

- getActivePage: This returns the current page.

In listing 9-5, a simple example of changePage is demonstrated:

```
Listing 9-5: test3.html
<div data-role="page" id="third">

    <div data-role="header">
        <h1>Test</h1>
    </div>

    <div role="main" class="ui-content">
    <input type="button" id="pageBtn" value="Go to page">
    </div>

</div>

<script>
$("#pageBtn").click(function() {
    $.mobile.pageContainer.pagecontainer("change",
    "test2.html",{transition:"flip"});
});
</script>
```

The page simply contains one button. At the bottom of the file is a jQuery event listener for that button. When clicked, the change method is used to load test2. html while making use of the flip transition.

Utilities related to path and URL

These utilities are related to the current location, URL, or path of the application:

- $.mobile.path.isAbsoluteUrl() and $.mobile.path.isRelativeUrl(): These two functions look at a URL and allow you to check whether they are either a full, absolute, or relative URL.

- $.mobile.path.get(): This returns the *directory* portion of a URL. So, given a URL in the http://www.raymondcamden.com/demos/foo.html form, it would return http://www.raymondcamden.com/demos/.

- `$.mobile.path.getDocumentBase()` and `$.mobile.path.getDocumentUrl()`: These return the base URL and full URL.

- `$.mobile.path.makeUrlAbsolute(relative url, absolute url)`: This is a slightly different form of the previous function. This utility works with absolute URLs instead.

The code in `Listing 9-6` is a *tester* application. It contains `form` fields, allowing you to test some of the methods previously discussed. First, let's just look at the UI controls used for the application:

```
Listing 9-6: test4.html
<div role="main" class="ui-content">

    <form>

    <div data-role="fieldcontain">
        <label for="isabsurl">Is Absolute URL?</label>
        <input type="text" name="isabsurl" id="isabsurl" value=""  />
        <div id="isabsurlresult"></div>
    </div>

    <div data-role="fieldcontain">
        <label for="isrelurl">Is Relative URL?</label>
        <input type="text" name="isrelurl" id="isrelurl" value=""  />
        <div id="isrelurlresult"></div>
    </div>

    <div data-role="fieldcontain">
        <label for="makeurl">Make URL Absolute</label>
        <input type="text" name="makeurl" id="makeurl"
        value="" placeholder="Relative URL" />
        <input type="text" name="makeurl2" id="makeurl2"
        value="" placeholder="Absolute URL" />
        <div id="makeurlresult"></div>
    </div>

    <div data-role="fieldcontain">
        <label for="pathget">Path Get</label>
        <input type="text" name="pathget" id="pathget" value=""  />
        <div id="pathgetresult"></div>
    </div>

    </form>
</div>
```

This creates the following form:

Now let's look at the following code:

```
Listing 9-7: test4.html (continued)
<script>
$("#isabsurl").keyup(function() {
    var thisVal = $(this).val();
    var isAbsUrl = $.mobile.path.isAbsoluteUrl(thisVal);
    $("#isabsurlresult").text(isAbsUrl);
});

$("#isrelurl").keyup(function() {
    var thisVal = $(this).val();
    var isRelUrl = $.mobile.path.isRelativeUrl(thisVal);
    $("#isrelurlresult").text(isRelUrl);
});
```

```
$("#makeurl,#makeurl2").keyup(function() {
    var urlVal1 = $("#makeurl").val();
    var urlVal2 = $("#makeurl2").val();
    var makeUrlResult = $.mobile.path.makeUrlAbsolute(urlVal1,urlVal2);
    $("#makeurlresult").text(makeUrlResult);
});

$("#pathget").keyup(function() {
    var thisVal = $(this).val();
    var path = $.mobile.path.get(thisVal);
    $("#pathgetresult").html(path);
});

</script>
```

The previous two code listings are a bit long, but they are really pretty simple. Each `fieldcontain` block consists of one particular test of the path methods and utilities. In the bottom half of the template, you can see that we've made use of the `keyup` event listeners to monitor changes to these fields and run each test. You can use this template to see how these methods react based on different inputs.

jQuery Mobile widget and form utilities

We've mentioned numerous times how jQuery Mobile automatically updates various items and supports things, such as lists and collapsible content. One of the things you may run into, however, is trying to get jQuery Mobile to work with the content loaded *after* the page is rendered. So, for example, imagine a `listview` that has data added to it via some JavaScript code. The code in Listing 9-8 demonstrates a simple example of this. It has a `listview` with a few items in it, and it also has a form by which a person could add new entries:

```
Listing 9-8: test5.html
<div data-role="page" id="third">

    <div data-role="header">
        <h1>List Updates</h1>
    </div>

    <div role="main" class="ui-content">

        <ul id="theList" data-role="listview" data-inset="true">
            <li>Initial</li>
            <li>Item</li>
        </ul>

        <form>
        <div data-role="fieldcontain">
```

```
        <label for="additem">New Item</label>
        <input type="text" name="additem" id="additem" value=""
/>
      </div>
      <input type="button" id="testBtn" value="Add It">
      </form>
    </div>

  </div>

  <script>
  $("#testBtn").click(function() {
    var itemToAdd = $.trim($("#additem").val());
    if(itemToAdd == "") return;
    $("#theList").append("<li>"+itemToAdd+"</li>");
  });
  </script>
```

When initially loaded, notice that everything seems fine. However, the following screenshot shows what happens when an item is added to the end of the list:

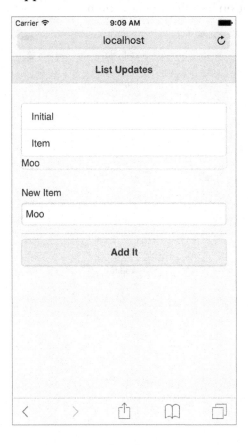

As you can see, the new item was indeed added to the end of the list, but it wasn't drawn correctly. This brings up a critical point. jQuery Mobile parses your code for data attributes and checks for form fields once. After it has done so, it considers its work done. Luckily, there is a standard way for these UI items to be updated. For `listview`, it is a simple matter of calling the `listview` method on the list itself. The `listview` method can be used to turn a new list into a `listview` or to refresh an existing `listview`. To refresh `listview`, we'd simply modify the code, as shown in the following code snippet:

```
<script>
  $("#testBtn").click(function() {
    var itemToAdd = $.trim($("#additem").val());
    if(itemToAdd == "") return;
    $("#theList").append("<li>"+itemToAdd+"</li>");
    $("#theList").listview("refresh");
  });
</script>
```

You can find the previous code snippet in `test6.html`. The following screenshot shows how the application handles the new item:

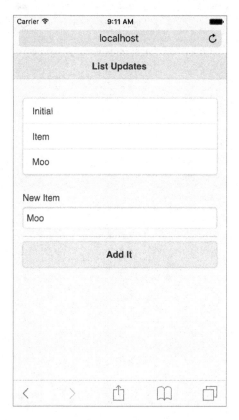

The `listview` method could also be used for completely new lists. Consider the following code snippet (`Listing 9-9`):

```
Listing 9-9: test7.html
<div data-role="page" id="third">

    <div data-role="header">
         <h1>List Updates</h1>
    </div>

    <div role="main" class="ui-content" id="contentDiv">

         <input type="button" id="testBtn" value="Add A List">
    </div>

</div>

<script>
$("#testBtn").click(function() {

    var html="<ul data-role='listview' data-inset='true'
id='theList'>"+
    "<li>Item One</li><li>Item Two</li></ul>";
    $("#contentDiv").append(html);
    $("#theList").listview();

});
</script>
```

In this example, a completely new list is appended to the `div` tag. Notice that we still include the proper `data-role`. But, this by itself is not enough. We follow up the HTML insertion with a call to the `listview` method to enhance the list that was just added.

Similar APIs exist for other fields. For example, new buttons added to a page can be enhanced by calling the `button()` method on them. In general, assume that any changes to the enhanced controls will need to be updated via their respective JavaScript APIs.

Summary

In this chapter, we (finally!) broke out some JavaScript. We looked at how you can configure various jQuery Mobile settings, what utilities exist, and how to handle postrendered updates to the enhanced controls.

In the next chapter, we'll continue working with JavaScript and look at the various events your code can listen to.

10
Working with Events

In this chapter, we will look at how events work in jQuery Mobile. While developers obviously have access to regular events (button clicks and so on), jQuery Mobile also exposes its own events for developers to make use of. These events are specifically focused on things that users typically do with a *touch* device. Supporting these events enables users to make use of the interactions they are already familiar with when working on a mobile device.

In this chapter, we will be covering the following topics:

- Touch, swipe, scroll, and other physical events
- Page events

Working with physical events

For the first part of this chapter, we will focus on the **physical** events or the events related to touch, and the other actions done with a device.

For those of you who have been testing jQuery Mobile using a regular browser, please note that some of the following examples will not work properly on a desktop browser. If you wish, you can download and install emulators for various mobile phone types. For example, Android has an SDK that supports creating virtual mobile devices. Apple also has a way to simulate an iOS device. Setting up and installing these emulators are beyond the scope of this chapter, but it is certainly an option. Of course, you can use a real hardware device as well.

Another option is to consider using the developer tools in your browser. Chrome, for example, lets you emulate touch events. See the DevTools documentation for more information.

Let's discuss the physical events that include the following:

- `tap` and `taphold`: The `tap` event represents what it sounds like—a quick physical touch on the web page. The `taphold` event is a longer touch. Many applications will make use of two separate actions—one for `tap` and one for `taphold`.

- `swipe`, `swipeleft`, and `swiperight`: These represent swipes or a finger movement across most of the devices. The `swipe` event is a generic one, whereas `swipeleft` and `swiperight` represent a swipe in a specific direction. There is no support for a swipe up or down event.

- `scrollstart` and `scrollstop`: They respectively handle the beginning and the end of scrolling a page.

- `orientationchange`: This is fired when the device's orientation changes.

The `vclick`, `vmousedown`, `vmouseup`, `vmousemove`, `vmousecancel`, and `vmouseover` events are **virtual** events meant to abstract away checking for either touch or mouse click events. As these are mainly just aliases for click and touch events, they will not be demonstrated.

Now that we've listed the basic physical events, let's start looking at a few examples. The code in `Listing 10-1` demonstrates a simple example of the `tap` and `taphold` events:

```
Listing 10-1: test1.html
<div data-role="page" id="first">

    <div data-role="header">
        <h1>Tap Tests</h1>
    </div>

    <div role="main" class="ui-content">

        <p>
            Tap anywhere on the page...
        </p>

        <p id="status"></p>

    </div>

</div>

<script>
$("body").bind("tap", function(e) {
```

```
        $("#status").text("You just did a tap event!");
    });

    $("body").bind("taphold", function(e) {
        $("#status").text("You just did a tap hold event!");
    });
</script>
```

This template is rather simple. The page has some explanatory text asking the user to tap on it. Beneath it is an empty paragraph. Note, though, the two binds at the end of the document. One listens for `tap`, while the other listens for `taphold`. The user can do either action and a different status message will be displayed. While being rather simple, this gives you a good idea on how you could respond differently based on how long the user holds his or her finger down. Note that a `taphold` event *also* fires a `tap` event, specifically when the user lifts his or her finger off the device. You will need to handle this behavior if you intend to use the `taphold` events.

Now, let's look at Listing 10-2, an example of `swipe` events:

```
Listing 10-2: test2.html
<div data-role="page" id="first">

    <div data-role="header">
        <h1>Swipe Tests</h1>
    </div>

    <div role="main" class="ui-content">

        <p>
            Swipe anywhere on the page...
        </p>

        <p id="status"></p>

    </div>

</div>

<script>
$("body").bind("swipe", function(e) {
    $("#status").append("You just did a swipe event!<br/>");
});

$("body").bind("swipeleft", function(e) {
    $("#status").append("You just did a swipe left event!<br/>");
```

```
});

$("body").bind("swiperight", function(e) {
    $("#status").append("You just did a swipe right event!<br/>");
});
</script>
```

This example is pretty similar to the previous one, except that now our event handlers listen for `swipe`, `swipeleft`, and `swiperight`. One important difference is that we append to the status `div` instead of simply setting it. Why? A `swiperight` or `swipeleft` event is automatically a `swipe` event. If we simply overwrote the text, the multiple events would event up overwriting each other. The following screenshot shows how the device looks after a few swipes:

How about a more complex example? Consider the following code snippet,
Listing 10-3:

```
Listing 10-3: test3.html
<div data-role="page" id="first">

    <div data-role="header">
        <h1>First</h1>
    </div>

    <div role="main" class="ui-content">

        <p>
            Swipe to navigate
        </p>

    </div>

</div>

<div data-role="page" id="second">

    <div data-role="header">
        <h1>Second</h1>
    </div>

    <div role="main" class="ui-content">

        <p>
            Swipe to the right...
        </p>
    </div>

</div>

<script>
$("body").bind("swipeleft swiperight", function(e) {
   var page = $.mobile.pageContainer.pagecontainer("getActivePage")
[0];

   var dir = e.type;
   if(page.id == "first" && dir == "swipeleft") {
        $.mobile.changePage("#second");
   }
```

```
    if(page.id == "second" && dir == "swiperight") {
        $.mobile.changePage("#first");
    }
});
</script>
```

In this example, we've got a file that includes two separate pages, one with the ID `first` and the other with the ID `second`. Notice that we have no links. So, how do we navigate? With swipes! Our event handler is now listening for both `swipeleft` and `swiperight`. We first grab the active page using `$.mobile.pageContainer.pagecontainer("getActivePage")`, as described in *Chapter 9, jQuery Mobile Configuration, Utilities, and JavaScript Methods*, on methods and utilities. In our preceding code, `[0]` at the end refers to the fact that the value is actually a jQuery selector. Using `[0]` grabs the actual DOM item. The event type will be either `swipeleft` or `swiperight`. Once we know this, we can actively move the user around depending on what page they are currently on and in what direction they swiped.

Now let's look at scrolling. You can detect when a scroll starts and when one ends. The code in `Listing 10-4` is another simple example of this in action:

```
Listing 10-4: test4.html
<div data-role="page" id="first">

    <div data-role="header">
        <h1>Scroll Tests</h1>
    </div>

    <div role="main" class="ui-content">

        <p>
            Scroll please....<br/>
            <br/>
            <br/>
            <br/>
            <br/>
            <br/>
            <br/>
        </p>

        <p id="status"></p>
    </div>

</div>
```

```
<script>
$("body").bind("scrollstart", function(e) {
    $("#status").append("Start<br/>");
});

$("body").bind("scrollstop", function(e) {
    $("#status").append("Done!<br/>");
});
</script>
```

This template is pretty similar to test1.html, the tap tester, except now we've listened to scrollstart and scrollstop. Also, note the list of <br/> tags. In the real source file, there are many of these. This will ensure that the page is actually scrollable when you test. When the scrolling starts and ends, we will simply append to another status div:

Now, let's look at the orientation events in Listing 10-5:

```
Listing 10-5: test5.html
<div data-role="page" id="first">

    <div data-role="header">
        <h1>Orientation Tests</h1>
    </div>

    <div role="main" class="ui-content">

        <p>
        Tilt this sideways!
        </p>

        <p id="status"></p>

    </div>

</div>

<script>
$(window).bind("orientationchange", function(e,type) {
    $("#status").html("Orientation changed to "+e.orientation);
});
</script>
```

The critical part of the previous code listing is the JavaScript at the end, specifically the event listener for changing the orientation. This is not actually a jQuery Mobile-supported event, but it is something supported by the browser itself. Once the event listener is attached, you can do whatever you wish based on the orientation of the device. The following screenshot demonstrates this:

Handling page events

Now that we've discussed physical type events, it's time to turn our attention to page container events. Remember that jQuery Mobile has its own concept of a page container that represents the space where pages are loaded and are working with the current page. In order to give developers even more control over how pages work within jQuery Mobile, numerous page events are supported. Not all will necessarily be useful in your day-to-day development. In general, page events can be split into the following categories:

- **Load**: These are events related to the loading of a page. They are `pagecontainerbeforeload`, `pagecontainerload`, and `pagecontainerloadfailed`. The `pagecontainerbeforeload` event is fired prior to a page being requested. Your code can either approve or deny this request based on whichever logic may make sense. If a page is loaded, then `pagecontainerload` is fired. Conversely, `pagecontainerloadfailed` will be fired on any load that does not complete.

- **Change**: These events are related to the change from one page to another. They are `pagecontainerbeforechange`, `pagecontainerchange`, and `pagecontainerchangefailed`. As before, the `pagecontainerbeforechange` function acts as a way to programmatically decline the event. If declined, the `pagecontainerchangefailed` event will be fired. The `pagebeforechange` event is fired *before* the `pagecontainerbeforeload` event. The `pagecontainerchange` event will be fired after the page is displayed.

- **Transition**: These events are related to the movement or transition from one page to another. They are `pagecontainerbeforeshow`, `pagecontainershow`, `pagecontainerbeforehide`, and `pagecontainerhide`. Both `pagecontainerbeforeshow` and `pagecontainerbeforehide` run prior to their related events but unlike `pagecontainerbeforeload` and `pagecontainerbeforechange`, they can't actually prevent the next event.

- **Init**: As it has been shown many times in this book, jQuery Mobile performs multiple updates to basic HTML to optimize it for mobile displays. These are initialization-related events. The events you can listen to are `pagebeforecreate` and `pagecreate`. The `pagebeforecreate` event fires before any of the automatic updates are fired on your controls. This allows you to manipulate your HTML beforehand via JavaScript. The `pagecreate` event is fired after the page content exists in the DOM, but before the layout is updated by jQuery Mobile. The official docs recommend this as the place to do any custom widget handling.

- **Remove**: There is one event for this category — `pagecontainerremove`. This event is fired before jQuery Mobile removes an inactive page from the DOM. You can listen to this event to prevent the framework from removing the page.

- **Layout**: The final category is related to layout and has one event — `updatelayout`. This is typically fired by other layout changes as a way to let the page know that it needs to update itself.

That's quite a lot! A simple way to look at these events in action would be to listen to all of them. In `Listing 10-6`, we have a simple example of this in action:

```
Listing 10-6: test_page.html
<div data-role="page" id="first">

    <div data-role="header">
        <h1>Page Event Tests</h1>
    </div>

    <div role="main" class="ui-content">
```

```
        <p>
        <a href="#page2" data-role="button">Go to Page 2</a>
        <a href="test_pagea.html" data-role="button">Go to Page 3</a>
        <a href="test_pageb.html" data-role="button">Go to Page 4</a>
        <a href="test_pageDOESNTEXIST.html" data-role="button">Go to
Page Failed</a>
        </p>

    </div>

</div>

<div data-role="page" id="page2">

    <div data-role="header">
        <h1>Page Event Tests</h1>
    </div>

    <div role="main" class="ui-content">

        <p>
        <a href="#first" data-role="button">Go to Page 1</a>
        <a href="test_pagea.html" data-role="button">Go to Page 3</a>
        <a href="test_pageb.html" data-role="button">Go to Page 4</a>
        </p>


    </div>

</div>

<script>

$(document).bind("pagecontainerbeforeload pagecontainerload
pagecontainerloadfailed pagecontainerbeforechange pagecontainerchange
pagecontainerchangefailed pagecontainerbeforeshow
pagecontainerbeforehide pagecontainershow pagecontainerhide
pagebeforecreate pagecreate pageremove updatelayout", function(e) {
    console.log(e.type);
});
```

This template is part of a four-page, three-file simple application that has buttons linking to each of the other pages. The other pages may be found in the ZIP file you downloaded. This demonstration uses the console API. A full explanation of the browser console wouldn't fit in this chapter, but you can think of it as a hidden debugging log useful for recording events and other messages. In this case, we've told jQuery to listen for all of our jQuery Mobile page events. We will then log the specific event type to the console. Click around a bit. The following screenshot shows how the console log looks using Safari's remote debug feature for the mobile simulator:

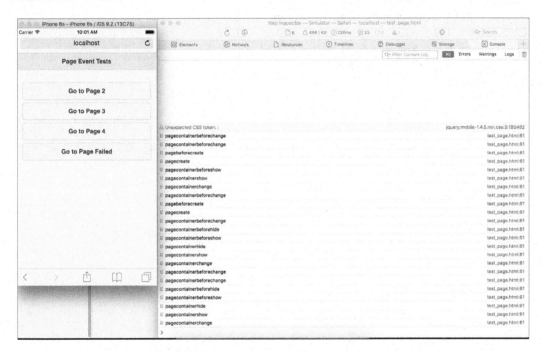

What about $(document).ready?

If you are a jQuery user, you may be curious how $(document).ready comes into play with a jQuery Mobile website. Almost all the jQuery applications use $(document).ready for initialization and other important setup operations. However, in a jQuery Mobile application, this will not work well. Since AJAX is used to load pages, $(document).ready is only really effective for the *first* page. Therefore, the pagecreate event should be used in cases where you would have used $(document).ready in the past.

Creating a real example

So, what about a real example? Our next set of code is going to demonstrate how to create a simple, but dynamic, jQuery Mobile website. The content will be loaded via AJAX. Normally, this would be dynamic data. But for our purposes, we'll use simple static files of the **JavaScript Object Notation (JSON)** data. JSON is a way to represent complex data as simple strings. The code in `Listing 10-7` is the application's home page:

```
Listing 10-7: test_dyn.html
<div data-role="page" id="homepage">

    <div data-role="header">
        <h1>Dynamic Pages</h1>
    </div>

    <div role="main" class="ui-content">

        <ul id="peopleList" data-role="listview" data-inset="true"></ul>


    </div>

</div>


<script>

$("#homepage").bind("pagebeforecreate", function(e) {
    //load in our people
    $.get("people.json", {}, function(res,code) {
        var s = "";
        for (var i = 0; i < res.length; i++) {
            s+="<li><a href='test_people.html?id="+res[i].id+"'>"+
            res[i].name+"</a></li>";
        }
        $("#peopleList").html(s).listview("refresh");
    }, "json");

});

$(document).on("pagecontainerbeforeshow", function(e) {
    console.log('pagecontainerbeforeshow');
```

```
    var page = $.mobile.pageContainer.pagecontainer("getActivePage")
[0];
    var parts = $.mobile.path.parseLocation();
    if(parts.pathname.indexOf("test_people") >= 0) {

        var thisId = parts.search.split("=")[1];
        $.get("person"+thisId+".json", {}, function(res, code) {
            $("h1",page).text(res.name);
            s = "<p>"+res.name+
            " is a "+res.gender+" and likes "+res.hobbies+"</p>";
            $("#contentArea", page).html(s);
        }, "json");


    }


});
</script>
```

The first thing you may notice about this jQuery Mobile page is that there isn't any actual content. Not within the jQuery Mobile page's content block, at least. There's listview but no actual content. So, where's the content going to come from? At the bottom of the page, you can see two event listeners. For now, let's just focus on the first one.

The code here binds to the pagebeforecreate event that jQuery Mobile fires for pages. We've told jQuery Mobile to run this event before it creates the page. This event will run once and only once. Within this event, we will use the jQuery get feature to do an AJAX request to the file people.json. This file is simply an array of names in the JSON format:

```
[{"id":1,"name":"Raymond Camden"},
{"id":2,"name":"Todd Sharp"},
{"id":3,"name":"Scott Stroz"},
{"id":4,"name":"Dave Ferguson"},
{"id":5,"name":"Adam Lehman"}]
```

Each name has both an ID and the actual name value. When loaded by jQuery, this is turned into an actual array of simple objects. Looking back at the event handler, you can see that we simply looped over this array and created a string representing a set of li tags. Note that each one has a link to test_people.html as well as a dynamic name. Also, note that the links themselves are dynamic. They include each person's ID value as retrieved from the JSON string.

It was mentioned earlier, but take note of the call to `listview("refresh")`:

```
$("#peopleList").html(s).listview("refresh");
```

Without the `listview("refresh")` portion, the items we added to `listview` would not be styled correctly.

Let's take a quick look at `test_people.html`:

```
Listing 10-8: test_people.html
<div data-role="page" id="personpage">

    <div data-role="header">
            <h1></h1>
    </div>

    <div role="main" class="ui-content" id="contentArea">

    </div>

</div>
```

As with our last page, this one is pretty devoid of content. Note that both the `header` and the content area are blank. But, if you remember the second event handler in `test_dyn.html`, you will know that we have support to load the content here. This time, we used the `pagecontainerbeforeshow` event. Why? We want to run this code before every display of the page. This will run for every `pagecontainershow` event, so we need to get the current page and the URL parts (via a helpful utility `parseLocation`), and see whether we're loading a person page versus the home page. This same data also contains the search value (query string) that we can parse to get a particular ID. Once we have this, we can then load in a particular JSON file for each person. The form of this filename is `personX.json`, where X is the number 1 through 5. The following line of code is an example:

```
{"name":"Raymond Camden","gender":"male","hobbies":"Star Wars"}
```

Obviously, a real person object would have a bit more data. Once we fetch this string, we can then parse it and lay out the result on the page itself:

Summary

In this chapter, we looked into events that jQuery Mobile applications can listen and respond to. These events include physical types (scrolling, orientation, and touching) and page-based ones as well.

In the next chapter, we'll look at how jQuery Mobile websites are themed—covering both out-of-the-box and custom themes as well.

11
Enhancing jQuery Mobile

In this chapter, you'll be learning how to enhance jQuery Mobile and how to make your mobile application really stand out from the pack by creating theme and icons to improve the look and functionality of your app. We will be covering the following topics:

- The building blocks of jQuery Mobile
- Creating your own jQuery Mobile theme using ThemeRoller

What's possible for designs?

The first reaction many developers have when they first use jQuery Mobile is awe at how easy it is to implement a rich, compelling mobile website for their users. The ease with which it converts plain HTML to beautiful, usable buttons, listviews, and form elements is a dream. The jQuery Mobile team shipped well-designed and attractive themes and commonly used icons along with the rest of the package. They even built a tool that allows developers to build out their own themes — **ThemeRoller** (`http://themeroller.jquerymobile.com`).

After working with jQuery Mobile for a time, some developers might ask, "What else can I do with this?", just like the muscle cars from the 60's and 70's. It wasn't enough that they were already awesome; the tweakers and the gearheads wanted to do more. If you identify with that mentality, then this chapter is for you.

The wonderful thing about jQuery Mobile is that it's just HTML. For this reason, we can do great things with very little effort. In this chapter, we'll be creating our own theme from scratch using ThemeRoller for jQuery Mobile. We'll be designing buttons from scratch and writing the CSS code needed to implement both low and high resolution versions. We'll also be looking at how we can expand on the styles and classes already available in jQuery Mobile and make something different and unique. Let's get started, shall we?

The visual building blocks of jQuery Mobile

As you've already seen, jQuery Mobile is very user-friendly and pleasing to the eye. It uses rounded corners, subtle gradients, and drop shadows to make elements stand out from their surroundings, and other tricks that graphic designers have been using for years in print. But on the Web, these effects were only possible with the use of images, or complicated and poorly supported plugins and applets.

With the advent of Web 2.0 and CSS3, all of these options have been made available to us, layman web developers. Just remember that with great power comes great responsibility. jQuery Mobile operates on the principle of progressive enhancement. A tricky phrase, but it just means that you should develop for the lowest common denominator and offer enhancements for browsers that understand it.

Lucky for us, these stylistic additions are almost purely cosmetic. If a browser doesn't understand the border-radius declaration, then it will simply display squared off corners. The same holds true for gradients and shadows. While jQuery Mobile adds these effects to your application out of the box, it's worthwhile to know how to add them on your own.

Border-radius

Rounded corners can be one of the most elegant and appealing effects, and it is also the simplest to add. There are a few caveats that developers need to know about this and the other effects. While there is a specification for border-radius as recommended by the W3C, it turns out that each of the primary browser manufacturers supports it in slightly different ways. The end result is the same, but the path to it varies. Let's take a look at the most basic border-radius declaration and its result:

```
#rounded {
  border-radius: 10 px;
}
```

The output of the preceding code is shown as follows:

This box has rounded corners.

You also have the option of rounding only certain corners as well as tweaking the values so that the corner isn't a perfect quarter-circle. Let's look at a few more examples:

```
#topLeftBottomRight {
  border-radius: 15px 0 15px 0;
}
```

The output of the preceding code is shown as follows:

Top left, bottom right

Let's take a look at another example:

```
#topLeft {
  border-top-left-radius: 100px 40px;
}
```

The output of the preceding code is shown as follows:

Top left

Applying drop shadows

Drop shadows in CSS take one of two forms: **text shadows** (applied to text) and **box shadows** (applied to everything else). Like `border-radius`, drop shadows are fairly straightforward if you're looking at the W3C specification.

Using text-shadow

Let's look at `text-shadow` first:

```
p {
  text-shadow: 2px 2px 2px #000000; /* horizontal, vertical, blur,
    color */
}
```

The output of the preceding code is shown as follows:

> The text in this paragraph will have a drop shadow that is offset 2 pixels to the right, 2 pixels
>
> to the bottom, is blurred by 2 pixels, and whose color is black.

This property also supports multiple shadows by adding additional declarations in a comma-separated list:

```
p {
    text-shadow: 0px 0 px 4px white,
    0 px -5px 4px #ffff33,
    2px -10 px 6px #ffdd33,
    -2px -15px 11px #ff8800,
    2px -25px 18px #ff2200
}
```

The output of the preceding code is shown as follows:

How about a cheesy fire effect!

Unlike the `border-radius` property, the `text-shadow` property doesn't require vendor prefixes. This doesn't mean that all the browsers support it; it simply means that browsers that support this property will display it as intended, while browsers that do not will simply see anything.

Using box-shadow

The `box-shadow` property follows a very similar model as `text-shadow` with one addition: the `inset` keyword that allows for inner shadowing. Let's go to the examples. First up is standard outer shadows:

```
#A {
box-shadow: -5px -5px #888888; /* horizontal, vertical, color */
}

#B {
```

```
box-shadow: -5px -5px 5px #888888; /* horizontal, vertical,
    blur, color */
}

#C {
box-shadow: 0 0 5px 5px #888888; /* horizontal, vertical, blur,
    spread, color */
}
```

The output of the preceding code is shown as follows:

Now check out these inner shadows. Snazzy, eh?

```
#D {
box-shadow: inset -5px -5px #888;}

#E {
box-shadow: inset 0px 0px 10 px 20px #888888;
}

#F {
box-shadow: inset 0 0 5px 5px #888888;
}
```

The output of the preceding code is shown as follows:

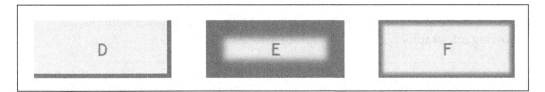

It's worth mentioning that both `box-shadow` and `text-shadow` can have their colors set with the less commonly used `rgb` and `rgba` declarations. This allows developers to set colors using the more familiar convention of RGB values. The `rgba` declaration also allows the setting of the color opacity from 0 to 1. The code for this has a simple change:

```
#opacity {
  box-shadow: inset 0 0 5px 5px rgb(0,0,0); /* black */
}
#transparent {
  box-shadow: inset 0 0 5px 5px rgba(0,0,0,.5); /* black with 50%
    opacity */
}
```

CSS gradients

CSS gradients are a great way to add beauty and impact to your website. The options include **linear gradients** (right to left, top to bottom, and so on) and **radial gradients** (moving outward from the center). By default, gradients consist of a start color and an end color. CSS gradients may also include additional tones using color stops.

It should be noted, however, that support for CSS gradients in older browsers isn't perfect, specifically Internet Explorer. The good news is that there are ways to address IE that can allow developers to reliably use gradients in their development. The bad news is that the code for this support is robust. Let's take a look at the simplest possible gradient declaration:

```
div {
  width: 500px;
  height: 100px;
  background: linear-gradient(left,  #ffffff 0%,#000000 100%);
}
```

Gradient declarations can be quite complex, so let's break it down with the following infographic:

DIRECTION: TOP, LEFT, 45DEG   STOP #1*   STOP #2*

LINEAR-GRADIENT(LEFT, #FFFFFF 0%,#000000 100%);

COLOR #1   COLOR #2

* INDICATES WHERE THE COLOR TRANSITION BEGINS/ENDS

Now here's the kicker. At the time of this writing, there were no browsers that supported the W3C specification using the actual property. Let's take a look at the code to support multiple browsers, and you'll love jQuery Mobile even more than you already do:

```
div {
  width: 500px;
  height: 100px;
  border: 1px solid #000000;
  /* Old browsers */
  background: #ffffff;
  /* FF3.6+ */
  background: -moz-linear-gradient(left,  #ffffff 0%, #000000
    100%);
  /* Chrome10+,Safari5.1+ */
  background: -webkit-linear-gradient(left,  #ffffff 0%,#000000
    100%);
  /* Opera 11.10+ */
  background: -o-linear-gradient(left,  #ffffff 0%,#000000 100%);
  /* IE10+ */
  background: -ms-linear-gradient(left,  #ffffff 0%,#000000 100%);
  /* W3C spec*/
  background: linear-gradient(left,  #ffffff 0%,#000000 100%);
  /* IE6-9 */
  filter: progid:DXImageTransform.Microsoft.gradient(
    startColorstr='#ffffff', endColorstr='#000000',GradientType=1
);
}
```

The output of the preceding code is shown as follows:

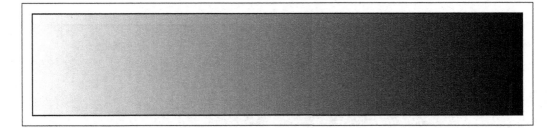

You can add multiple colors to your gradient by adding additional comma-separated declarations. Consider the following code:

```
div {
  width: 500px;
  height: 100px;
  border: 1px solid #000000;
  /* Old browsers */
  background: #ffffff;
  /* FF3.6+ */
  background: -moz-linear-gradient(left,  #ffffff 0%, #000000 35%,
    #a8a8a8 100%);
  /* Chrome10+,Safari5.1+ */
  background: -webkit-linear-gradient(left,  #ffffff 0%,#000000
    35%,#a8a8a8 100%);
  /* Opera 11.10+ */
  background: -o-linear-gradient(left,  #ffffff 0%,#000000
    35%,#a8a8a8 100%);
  /* IE10+ */
  background: -ms-linear-gradient(left,  #ffffff 0%,#000000
    35%,#a8a8a8 100%);
  /* W3C */
  background: linear-gradient(left,  #ffffff 0%,#000000
    35%,#a8a8a8 100%);
  /* IE6-9 */
  filter: progid:DXImageTransform.Microsoft.gradient(
    startColorstr='#ffffff', endColorstr='#a8a8a8',GradientType=1
    );
}
```

The previous code results in the following gradient:

As you might guess after reading the last few pages, jQuery Mobile does a lot of heavy lifting on your behalf. Not only does it add slick gradients as page backgrounds, but it has to also keep track of all of the browser quirks that might prevent that sweet drop shadow from showing up. As we move into the next section, you'll likely be even more impressed with the way it handles themes and color swatches.

The basics of jQuery Mobile theming

Theming in jQuery Mobile is straightforward and simple to use for the developer, but it is pretty elaborate behind the scenes. Luckily, there will rarely be a time when you need to know everything that's being done for you. However, it's worth a little bit of our time to understand how it works.

Out of the box, jQuery Mobile comes with a theme set comprising two color swatches, each associated with a letter (A and B). The theme contains a series of base CSS classes that can be applied at will to nearly any element and contain global settings for width, height, border radius, and shadows. The individual swatches contain specific information about color, fonts, and so on.

Additional swatches can be added to the original swatches from C to Z, or the original swatches can be replaced or overridden at will. This system allows for a total of 26 distinct swatches, allowing for millions of possible combinations of theme colors, styles, and patterns. You apply a jQuery Mobile theme to the selected element by adding a `data-theme` attribute with the letter of the desired theme, as shown in the following screenshot:

Developers will generally choose to use the `data-theme` attribute method when applying styles, but it's also possible to attach the CSS class names directly to your page elements for more granular control. There are a handful of primary prefixes that allow for this flexibility.

Bars (.ui-bar-?)

The bar prefix is generally applied to headers, footers, and other areas of high importance:

Content blocks (.ui-body-?)

Content blocks are generally applied to areas where paragraph text is expected to occur. Their color helps to ensure maximum readability with the text color placed against them:

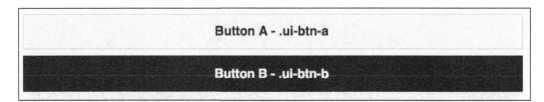

Buttons and listviews (.ui-btn-?)

Buttons and listviews are two of the most important elements in the jQuery Mobile library, and you can be rest assured that the team took their time getting these right:

Mixing and matching swatches

One of the nice things about theming in jQuery Mobile is that child elements inherit from their parent, unless otherwise specified. This means that if you put a button without its own `data-theme` attribute inside a header or footer bar, this button will use the same theme as its parent. Wicked, eh? Let's take a look at an example that illustrates this:

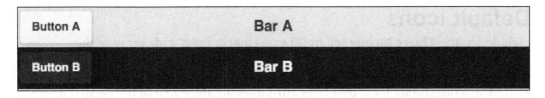

It's also perfectly acceptable and even encouraged to place an element using one swatch as the child of an element using another swatch. This can help the element stand out more, match a different part of the app, or whatever reasoning the developer chooses. It's possible, and what's more, it's easy. Simply place a button (or another element) inside a header bar, and assign it its own `data-theme` attribute:

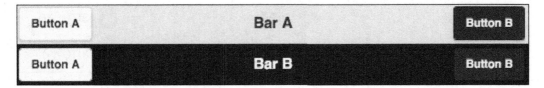

Site-wide active state

jQuery Mobile also applies a global active state for all the elements. This active state is used for buttons, form elements, navigation, and anywhere there's a need to indicate that something is currently selected. The only way to change this color value is to set (or override) it via CSS. The CSS class for the active state is appropriately named `.ui-btn-active`:

Default icons

Included in the jQuery Mobile set are 20 icons that cover a wide array of the developers' needs. The icon set is white on transparent that jQuery Mobile overlays over a semitransparent black circle to provide contrast against all of the swatches. To add an icon, specify the `data-icon` attribute with the name of the desired icon. In addition to the white icon that is set, there is also a black on transparent icon set for colors that need higher contrast. You can find the full list of icons at the jQuery Mobile documentation page (`http://api.jquerymobile.com/icons/`), and they cover what you would expect in an application: a home icon, directional icons, and the other icons used in mobile apps. Here is a small sample of these icons:

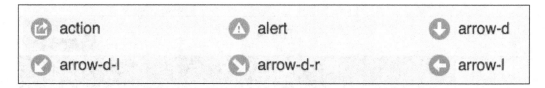

jQuery Mobile also provides the ability to place icons at the top or bottom or on the left- or right-hand side of a button using the `data-iconpos="[top, right, bottom, left]"` attribute with left being the default placement. Developers are also able to display an icon alone, without text, by specifying `data-iconpos="notext"`:

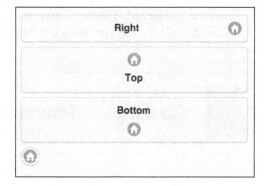

Customized icons are also possible and will be covered later in this chapter.

Creating and using a custom theme

We already discussed how powerful theming is in jQuery Mobile. It makes it trivial to develop a rich mobile website with simple and elegant styles. Even more powerful is the ability to create your own library of swatches that can be used to make your application or website truly unique. Developing your own theme can be approached in one of the two ways:

1. Download and open the existing jQuery Mobile CSS file and edit to your heart's content.

2. Point your web browser to ThemeRoller for jQuery Mobile (`http://themeroller.jquerymobile.com`).

We'll be focusing solely on the second option, because let's be honest, why should you wade through all of that CSS when you can point, click, and drag your way to a new theme full of swatches in 10 minutes? Let's find out what ThemeRoller is all about.

What's ThemeRoller?

ThemeRoller for jQuery Mobile is an extension of a web-based app that was written for the jQuery UI project. It allows users to quickly assemble a theme full of swatches in minutes by pointing, clicking, and dragging. It features an interactive preview so that you can immediately see how your changes affect your theme. It also has a built-in inspector tool that helps you dig into the minute details (should you want them). It also integrates with Adobe® Kuler®, a color management tool. You can download your theme after you're done, you can share it with others via a custom URL, and you can reimport past themes for last-minute tweaking. It's a powerful tool and is a perfect complement to jQuery Mobile.

One of the hallmarks of the five default swatches is that the jQuery Mobile team spent quite a bit of time working on readability and usability. Within a single theme, the areas that have the most contrast are the areas that are most prominent on the page. This includes the header (and the `listview` headers) and buttons. When creating your own theme, it's a good idea to keep this in mind. We always focus on usability within our app, right? What good is a slick app if no one can read it because of poor color choices.

Using ThemeRoller

The first thing you'll see when you load ThemeRoller is a slick-looking splash screen, as shown in the following screenshot:

Following the splash screen is a helpful getting started screen (the getting started screen has some helpful tips, so make sure you glance at it before clicking on the **Get Rolling** button):

Welcome to ThemeRoller for jQuery Mobile

Create up to 26 theme "swatches" lettered from A-Z, each with a unique color scheme, then mix and match for unlimited possibilities.

To upgrade a theme to 1.4.5: Click the Import button, paste in your uncompressed theme, then tweak and download the upgraded version.

Get Rolling

After all of the splash screens are out of the way, you'll be presented with the primary interface, as follows:

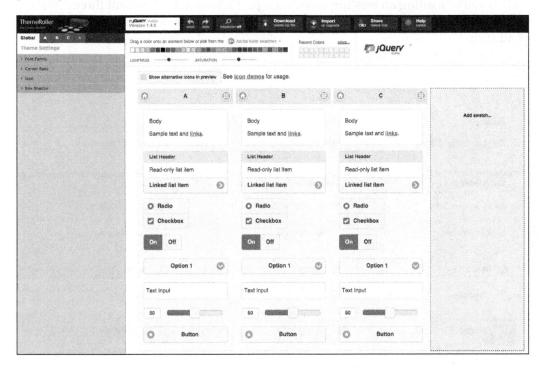

ThemeRoller is broken up into four main areas: preview, color, inspector, and tools. Each of these contains important functionality that we need to review. We'll start with the preview section.

Preview

Unless you're loading an existing theme, the preview area will present three complete, identical, and interactive jQuery Mobile pages packed with widgets of all sorts:

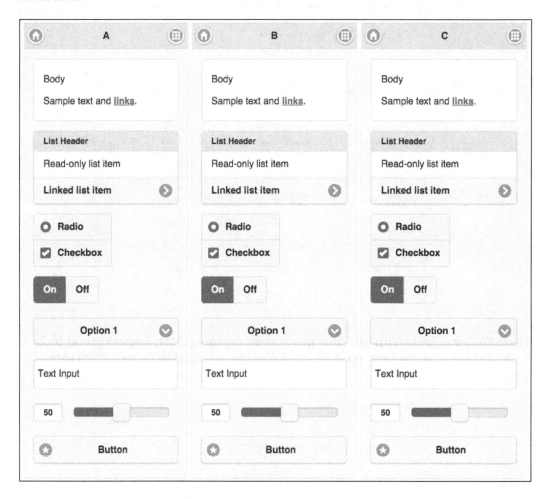

Move your mouse over them and you'll see that each page is functional. The header on each page contains a letter indicating which swatch controls its appearance.

Colors

At the top of the page, you'll see a series of color chips along with two slider controls and a toggle button. Further to the right, you'll see 20 blank chips. These will contain your recently used colors and will be empty until you've selected a color.

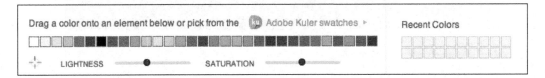

Below the color chips are two sliders labeled **Lightness** and **Saturation**. The **Lightness** slider adjusts the light and dark tones of the series of color swatches, while the **Saturation** slider makes the colors more or less vibrant. Taken together, a user should be able to approximate nearly any color they choose. To use colors from Kuler®, click on the text link marked **Adobe Kuler swatches**.

Each of the color chips can be dragged onto any element within the preview area. This makes the development of a swatch set extremely easy. Note that many of the jQuery Mobile styles overlap; for example, the header bar at the top of the page receives the same style as the header of listview. Adjust the colors as desired and then drag each chip onto an element on the page.

Remember that each individual page is its own swatch, so be careful about how you choose to mix colors.

Inspector

On the far left-hand side of the interface is the **Inspector** panel that allows you to exercise fine-grain control over your theme.

The bottom section contains a series of tabs labeled **Global**, **A**, **B**, **C**, and **+**. Each tab contains an accordion panel with all of the values for an individual swatch, except for the **Global** tab that applies to all of the swatches.

Additional swatches can be added to your theme in two ways. Clicking on the **+** tab at the top of **Inspector** adds a new swatch at the last place in your theme. You can also add a new swatch by clicking on the **Add swatch...** button located at the bottom of the preview area. Swatches can be deleted by selecting the tab with the swatch you want to remove and then clicking on the **Delete** link located to the right of the swatch name.

Note that deleting a swatch from the top of the stack will cause the remaining swatches to be renamed.

Tools

At the top of the page is a series of buttons. These buttons allow you to perform a variety of tasks, which we'll cover in a moment. But first, let's take a closer look at the buttons themselves:

You'll notice the following buttons: a switch that allows you to change between the current and previous versions, **undo/redo**, and a toggle button for **Inspector**. Setting this toggle to **on** allows you to inspect any of the widgets in the preview area. Hovering over a widget highlights that element with a blue box. Clicking on the element will cause the accordion menu in the **Inspector** area to expand to display settings specific to that element.

There are four additional buttons that allow you to download your theme, import, or upgrade a previously created theme, and share your theme with others. There is also a **Help** button for people who didn't buy this book!

Creating a theme for Notekeeper

Now that we're familiar with the ThemeRoller interface, how about we go ahead and create our first theme? Rather than building one in abstract, let's create one that we'll actually use for the Notekeeper app we built earlier. Let's start simple by modifying one of the existing themes that ship with jQuery Mobile. The team was kind enough to let users import the default themes as a starting place for new themes, so that's where we'll head first. Click on the **Import** button at the top of the window and you'll get a box allowing you to paste in the contents of an existing theme:

Import the default theme by clicking on the link appropriately titled **Import Default Theme** in the top-right corner. After the text area fills with CSS, click on **Import**. The preview area will reload and display swatches **A** and **B**.

We'll focus our efforts on changing the white swatch, **A**, as it's closest to what our end goal is. Just to keep things clean, go ahead and delete **Swatch B**:

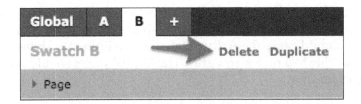

This swatch looks nice, but it's a little bland. Let's inject a little color by changing the header to a nice green. The simplest way to determine what values should be changed for any element is to use **Inspector**. Toggle the **Inspector** tool at the top and then click anywhere on the header of theme **A**. You'll know you got it right if the **A** tab is selected on the left-hand side and the **Header/Footer Bar** panel expands:

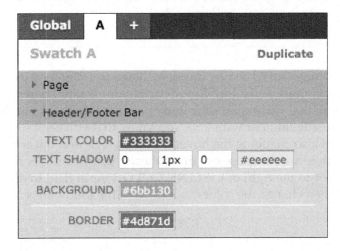

You can change the color in one of the following ways. You can drag a color chip from the top directly onto the background. You can also drag a color chip onto an input field. Finally, you can manually input the value. Notice that when you click on a field containing a color value, you're provided with a slick color picker. Go ahead and change the values in the input fields in this panel to the values shown in the preceding screenshot.

It is looking good, but now, the blue from the theme's active state is clashing with our green. Using the **Inspector** tool, click once on the **On** section of the **On/Off** toggle bar. This should cause the **Active State** panel within the **Global** tab to expand. We'll change the blue to a nice warm grey. The **Global** panel should now look like the following screenshot:

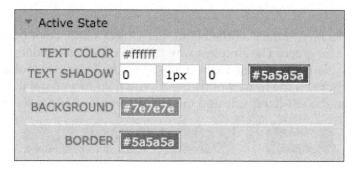

There's only one thing that's keeping our new theme from looking its best: the blue text link in the paragraph at the top. Going back to our trusty **Inspector**, let's click directly on the link that will expand the **Body** panel within the **A** tab. Now, for those who are already familiar with CSS, you know that you can't simply change the link color without also changing the hover, visited:hover, and the active states. The problem is that there are no options to make these changes, but ThemeRoller has you covered. Click on **+** to the right of the **LINK COLOR** input field to display the rest of the options and then change the colors, as shown in the following screenshot:

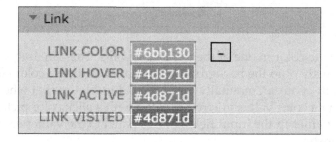

That's it! Feel free to make additional changes to your theme as you explore the **Inspector** area. Change whatever you like; it's just bits and bytes right now.

Exporting your theme

Now that we've finished our theme, we're going to export it for use in our Notekeeper application. This is a straightforward process that begins by clicking on the **Download** button located in the middle of the page at the top of the interface. You'll be presented with a box allowing you to name your theme, some information on how to apply your theme, and a button labeled **Download Zip**. After naming our theme `Notekeeper`, click on the **Download Zip** button, and you'll receive a tasty little morsel in your `Downloads` folder.

Extract the contents of the ZIP file and you'll see the following directory structure:

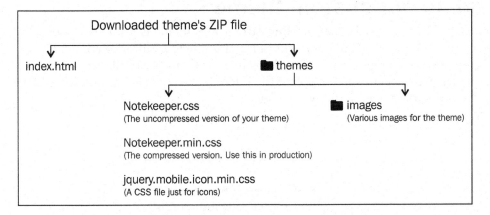

The HTML file at the top of the tree contains information on how to implement your theme as well as a few widgets to confirm that the theme works. In order to test your theme, you will need to copy the files to a web server and then open the `index.html` file.

 A few notes about the download and the implementation of themes are: the jQuery team provides the icons for buttons in this ZIP file for a reason. The theme requires these images to be relative to the CSS file. This means that unless you're already using the default theme, you need to also include the `images` folder when you upload your theme to your website, or the icons won't show up.

Hang on to the uncompressed version of your theme: While you won't want to use it in production because of the size, you will need it should you ever wish to edit it within ThemeRoller. ThemeRoller cannot import the minified CSS file.

Updating the Notekeeper app

It's time for us to tie all of these loose ends together. We have a custom theme that we built using ThemeRoller, and now, it's time for us to put all the pieces together. You'll need the following pieces to finish up:

- The code you completed at the end of *Chapter 8, Moving Further with the Notekeeper Mobile Application*
- The custom theme you created earlier in this chapter

Adding our custom theme

Let's start with the easiest part. Adding our custom theme is pretty simple. Open `notekeeper.html` (in your browser and in the text editor of your choice). Additionally, open the `index.html` file from your theme's ZIP file. We're going to merge the `<head>` tag from the theme file into `notekeeper.html`. You can see the results of the merge in the following code:

```
<title>Notekeeper</title>
<meta name="viewport"
      content="width=device-width, initial-scale=1">

<link rel="stylesheet" href="themes/Notekeeper.min.css" />
<link rel="stylesheet" href="themes/jquery.mobile.icons.min.css" />
<link rel="stylesheet" href =
"http://code.jquery.com/mobile/1.4.5/jquery.mobile.structure-
1.4.5.min.css" />

<link rel="stylesheet" href="styles.css" />

<script type="text/javascript"
        src="http://code.jquery.com/jquery-2.1.3.min.js">
</script>

<script type="text/javascript"
        src="http://code.jquery.com/mobile/1.4.5/jquery.mobile-
1.4.5.min.js">
</script>
<script src="application.js"></script>
```

The first new line implements the new theme we created. Even with a rich theming system, such as the one jQuery Mobile has, we're going to have some custom CSS for various things. The `styles.css` file is where the custom CSS styles will go. But for now, it will be blank.

Go ahead and reload your browser window and take a look at your new theme in action:

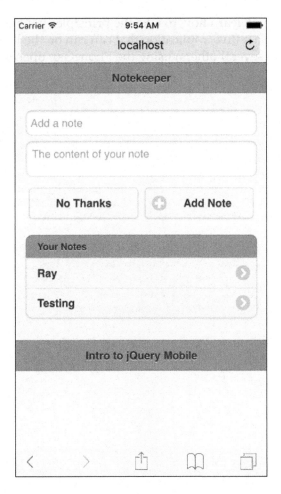

Isn't it snazzy?

Summary

In this chapter, you learned about advanced CSS techniques that are central to the jQuery Mobile experience, and how jQuery Mobile uses them to provide a rich interface to the end user. We took a deep dive into the basics of jQuery Mobile theming and how it works. We built a custom theme using the ThemeRoller tool and you learned how to implement it in our application.

In the next chapter, you'll learn how to take the principles you've learned in the past 11 chapters and create a native application that can run on the iOS and Android platforms (along with several others) using the PhoneGap open source library.

12
Creating Native Applications

In this chapter, we will look at how to turn jQuery Mobile-based web applications into native applications for mobile devices. We'll discuss the PhoneGap framework and how it allows you to tap into your device's hardware.

In this chapter, we will cover the following topics:

- The PhoneGap project and what it does
- How to use PhoneGap's Build service to create native applications

HTML as a native application

For most folks, creating a native application on a platform, such as Android or iOS, requires learning an entirely new programming language. While it is always good to learn new languages and expand your skill set, wouldn't it be cool if you could take your existing HTML skills and use them natively on a mobile device?

Luckily, there is one such platform PhoneGap (http://www.phonegap.com), which is an open source project that allows you to take HTML pages and create native applications. This code is entirely free and can be used to develop applications for iOS (both iPhone and iPad), Android (again both phones and tablets), Blackberry, WebOS, Windows Phone 7, Windows Phone 8, Symbian, and Bada. PhoneGap works by creating a project in the native environment and pointing to an HTML file. Once it is set up, you can use your existing HTML, CSS, and JavaScript skills to create the UI and the functionality of your application.

Even better, PhoneGap provides additional APIs to your JavaScript code. These APIs include the following:

- **Accelerometer**: This allows your code to detect basic movement on the device
- **Camera**: This allows your code to work with the camera
- **Compass**: This gives you access to the compass on the device
- **Connection**: This lets your application determine whether your user is online, and if so, what type of connection is supported
- **Contacts**: This provides basic search and contact creation support
- **Device**: This provides basic device metadata, such as the operating system
- **Events**: This comprises various types of events
- **File**: This provides read/write access to the device's storage
- **Geolocation**: This provides a way to detect the location of the device
- **Globalization**: This automatically formats numbers and dates in your user's locale
- **Media**: This allows for basic audio/video capture support
- **Network**: This determines the network connectivity settings of the device
- **Notification**: This is a simple way to create a notification (via a popup, sound, or vibration)
- **Storage**: This provides access to a simple SQL database

By using these APIs, you can take normal HTML websites and turn them into powerful native-like applications that users can download and install on their devices.

Before we go any further, you should know that PhoneGap is an implementation of Apache Cordova. PhoneGap is Adobe's implementation, but for all intents and purposes, it is the same thing. Since most people know about PhoneGap, we will use it in the book. At the end of the day, do not forget that Cordova is an open source that is free and available to all.

Working with PhoneGap

Creating a PhoneGap project is done via two main methods. The primary way people use PhoneGap is by using a command-line tool and the SDKs of the platform they are planning to support. PhoneGap also supports a desktop application for folks not comfortable with the **command line interface (CLI)**.

 The PhoneGap documentation (`http://docs.phonegap.com`) provides details on how to use either.

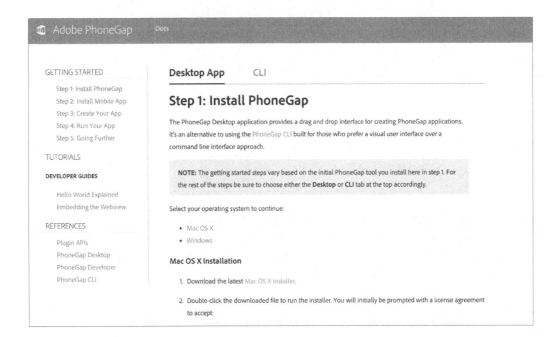

This chapter is on the other option for creating native applications, the **PhoneGap Build** service. PhoneGap Build (`https://build.phonegap.com`) is an online service that simplifies and automates the process of creating native applications. It allows you to simply upload code (or use a public source control repository) to generate native binaries. Even better, you can use PhoneGap Build to generate binaries for all their supported platforms. This means that you can write your code once and spit out code for iOS, Android, Blackberry, and other platforms, all from the website itself:

The PhoneGap Build service is not free, though. Pricing plans and other details may be found on the website, but luckily, there is a free developer plan. That is the service we'll be using for this chapter. You can sign up with either an Adobe ID or GitHub credentials. After signing up, you can create your first PhoneGap Build project.

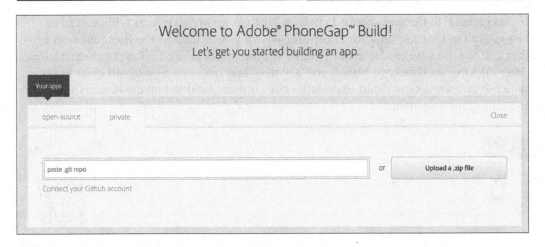

Notice that the Build service supports seeding a project from an existing GitHub repository or via an uploaded ZIP file. At this point, let's switch away from the website and back to the code. We want to begin with a very simple set of code. Later on, in the chapter, we will do something a bit more interesting. But for now, our objective is to just upload some HTML and see what comes next. In the code you downloaded from GitHub, open the `c12` folder and look at the `app1` folder. This contains a copy of one of the list examples from *Chapter 4, Working with Lists*. It uses jQuery Mobile to create a simple list of four people along with thumbnail pictures. Nothing too exciting, but it gets the job done for our purposes here.

It has one big difference from the original file. Instead of loading jQuery and jQuery Mobile from the CDN, local copies are used. Mobile apps could be run when users are offline or in a poor reception area. By using the libraries locally, you ensure your app runs even in adverse network conditions.

You will notice that there is already an `app1.zip` file.

If you go back to the website and click on **Upload an archive**, you will be able to browse to the location on your computer where you extracted the files and select that ZIP file. Be sure to also enter a name for the application; I chose FirstBuildApp. After clicking on **Ready to build**, you are then taken to a page with all your apps, which if you are a new Build user, will only contain the one just created, as shown in the following screenshot:

Clicking on the app title then gives you the option to download various flavors of the application. Believe it or not, you are already able to download a version for most platforms. Working with iOS requires you to provide a certificate. If you create a certificate (that must be done on a Mac), you can upload it to PhoneGap Build and tell it to use the certificate for iOS builds. What's cool is that once you've done that, you can use a Windows machine (or even a Linux machine) to work on your HTML, upload to PhoneGap Build, and create iOS builds. Click on the application title to go to the application's detail page, as shown in the following screenshot:

Note that you can now download (again, you will need a certificate for iOS) by simply clicking on the link next to your platform.

Actually, using the applications depends on your platform of choice. For Android, you need to ensure that you have enabled the **Allow installation of non-Market applications** setting. The exact wording and location of that setting will depend on your device. You can sign the application by editing the settings on the PhoneGap Build website. Once you've done this, you can actually submit your application to the Android market. Since Android allows you to play with applications that are not signed, you can skip this step while testing. The following screenshot shows the application running on an Android emulator:

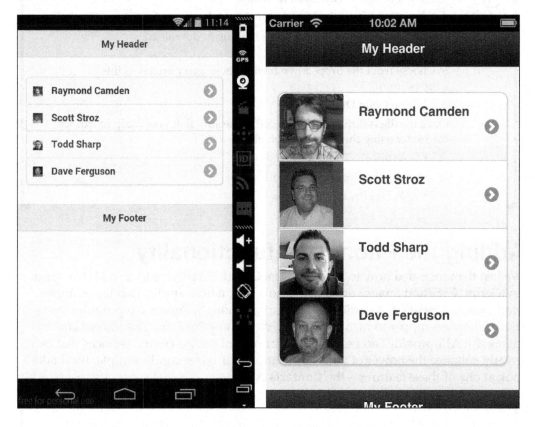

Downloading the example code

You can download the example code files for this book from your account at http://www.packtpub.com. If you purchased this book elsewhere, you can visit http://www.packtpub.com/support and register to have the files e-mailed directly to you.

You can download the code files by following these steps:

1. Log in or register to our website using your e-mail address and password.
2. Hover the mouse pointer on the **SUPPORT** tab at the top.

3. Click on **Code Downloads & Errata**.
4. Enter the name of the book in the **Search** box.
5. Select the book for which you're looking to download the code files.
6. Choose from the drop-down menu where you purchased this book from.
7. Click on **Code Download**.

Once the file is downloaded, please make sure that you unzip or extract the folder using the latest version of:

- WinRAR/7-Zip for Windows
- Zipeg/iZip/UnRarX for Mac
- 7-Zip/PeaZip for Linux

Adding the PhoneGap functionality

We just demonstrated how to use the PhoneGap Build service to turn HTML (and JavaScript, CSS, and images of course) into a real, native application for multiple platforms. As mentioned earlier in the chapter, though, PhoneGap provides more than a simple wrapper to turn HTML into native applications. The PhoneGap JavaScript API provides access to a number of cool device-centric services that can greatly enhance the power of your application. For our second example, we'll take a look at one of these features—the **Contacts API**.

For full details, see the Contacts API documentation that is available at
`https://www.npmjs.com/package/cordova-plugin-contacts`.

The application in `Code 12-1` is a simple `Contact Search` tool. Let's take a look at the code and then cover what's going on:

```
Code 12-1: index.html
<!DOCTYPE html>
<html>
<head>
<title>Contact Search</title>
<meta name="viewport"
      content="width=device-width, initial-scale=1">
<link rel="stylesheet"
      href="css/jquery.mobile-1.4.5.min.css" />
<script type="text/javascript"
        src="js/jquery-2.1.3.min.js">
</script>
<script type="text/javascript"
        src="js/jquery.mobile-1.4.5.min.js">
</script>
<script src="phonegap.js"></script>
<script>
document.addEventListener("deviceready", onDeviceReady, false);

function onDeviceReady(){

    $("#searchButton").on("touchend", function() {
        var search = $.trim($("#search").val());
        if(search == "") return;

        var opt = new ContactFindOptions();
        opt.filter = search;
        opt.multiple = true;
        navigator.contacts.find(["displayName","emails"],
foundContacts, errorContacts, opt);
    });

    foundContacts = function(matches){
        //create results in our list
        var s = "";
        for (var i = 0; i < matches.length; i++) {
            s += "<li>"+matches[i].displayName+"</li>";
        }
        $("#results").html(s);
```

```
            $("#results").listview("refresh");
    }

    errorContacts = function(err){
          navigator.notification.alert(
"Sorry, we had a problem and gave up.", function() {});
    }
}

</script>
</head>

<body>

<div data-role="page">

        <div data-role="header">
            <h1>Contact Search</h1>
        </div>

        <div role="main" class="ui-content">

          <input type="search" id="search" value=""  />
              <button id="searchButton">Search</button>

          <ul id="results"
          data-role="listview" data-inset="true"></ul>

        </div>


    </div>

</div>

</body>
</html>
```

Let's begin by looking at the layout portion of the application that resides in the bottom half of the file. You can see your jQuery Mobile page structure, and within it, an input field, a button, and an empty list. The idea here is that the user will enter a name to search for and hit the button, and the results will show up within the list. The following screenshot demonstrates the output:

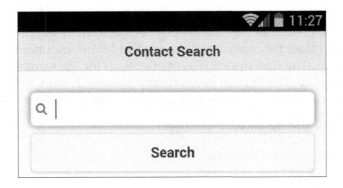

Now take a look at the JavaScript code. The first change we've made is to include the PhoneGap JavaScript library:

```
<script src="phonegap.js"></script>
```

You may be wondering why this file? You don't need it! When you upload your code to PhoneGap Build, the service automatically injects the proper JavaScript file for the platform. This code provides access to various device features, such as the Contacts database.

The next interesting tidbit is the following line of code:

```
document.addEventListener("deviceready", onDeviceReady, false);
```

The deviceready event is a special event fired by PhoneGap. It essentially | means that your code can now make use of advanced functionality, such as the Contacts API.

Within the onDeviceReady event handler, we have a few things going on. The first function of note is the event handler for the **Search** button. The first few lines simply get, trim, and validate the value.

After we are sure there's actually something to search for, you can see the first actual use of the Contacts API, as shown in the following code snippet:

```
var opt = new ContactFindOptions();
opt.filter = search;
opt.multiple = true;
navigator.contacts.find(["displayName","emails"], foundContacts,
  errorContacts, opt);
```

The Contacts API has a search method. Its first argument is an array of fields to both search and return. In our case, we are saying that we want to search against the name and e-mail values for contacts. The second and third arguments are the success and error callbacks. The final option is a set of options for the search. You can see it created before the call. The `filter` key is simply the search term. By default, contact searches return one result, so we will specifically ask for multiple results as well.

Now let's take a look at the success handler:

```
foundContacts = function(matches){
    //create results in our list
    var s = "";
    for (var i = 0; i < matches.length; i++) {
        s += "<li>"+matches[i].displayName+"</li>";
    }
    $("#results").html(s);
    $("#results").listview("refresh");
}
```

The result of **Contact Search** will be an array of results. Remember that you only get back what you asked for, so our result objects contain the `displayName` and `emails` properties. For now, our code simply takes `displayName` and adds it to the list. Remembering what was taught in one of the previous chapters, we also know that we need to refresh jQuery Mobile `listview` whenever we modify it. The following screenshot shows a sample search:

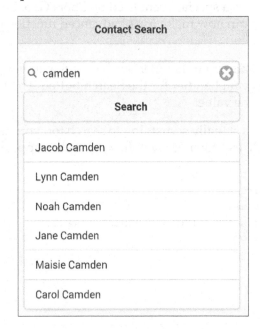

There's one more change that PhoneGap Build requires. In order to support working with `Contacts`, you have to tell the service to include the plugin that supports it. This is done via a `config.xml` file included in the source code for this book.

 You can read more about how this file works on the PhoneGap Build website (`http://docs.build.phonegap.com/en_US/ configuring_basics.md.html#The%20Basics`).

Summary

In this chapter, we looked into the PhoneGap open source project, and how it allows you to take your HTML, JavaScript, and CSS, and create native applications for a multitude of different devices. We played with the Build service and used it to upload our code and download compiled native applications. While jQuery Mobile isn't required with PhoneGap, the two make an incredibly powerful team.

In the next chapter, we'll take this team and create our final application, a full-fledged RSS reader.

13
Becoming an Expert – Building an RSS Reader Application

Now that you've been introduced to jQuery Mobile and its features, it's time to build our final, full application—an RSS reader.

In this chapter, we will be covering the following topics:

- The RSS reader application and its features
- How to create the application
- What could be added to the application

RSS reader – the application

Really Simple Syndication (RSS) is a way for websites to create a computer-readable index of their information. Using a common XML format, websites can let people read their content via other websites and applications. RSS is most popular on blog and news websites.

Before diving into the code, it may make sense to quickly demonstrate the application in its final working form, so you can see the pieces and how they work together. The RSS reader application is an application meant to take RSS feeds (for example, from CNN, ESPN, and other websites), parse them into readable data, and provide a way for the user to view the articles. This application will allow you to add and delete feeds, providing both a name and a URL, and then provide a way to view the current entries from the feed.

The application begins with a basic set of instructions. These instructions are only visible when you run the application without any known feeds, as shown in the following screenshot:

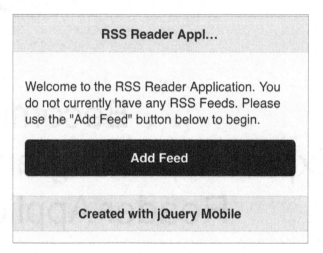

Clicking on the **Add Feed** button brings you to a simple form, allowing for both a name and a URL .Unfortunately, the URL has to be typed in manually. Luckily, modern mobile devices allow for copy and paste. I'd strongly recommend using this.

After adding the feed, you are redirected to the home page. The following screenshot shows the view after a few feeds are added:

To begin reading entries, the user simply selects one of the feeds. This will then fetch the feed and display the current entries, as shown in the following screenshot:

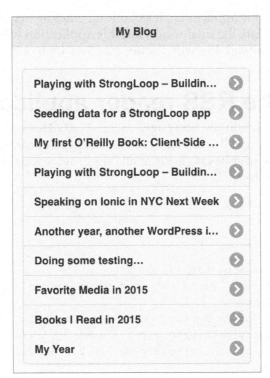

The final part of the application is the entry view itself. Some blogs don't provide a full copy of the entry via RSS, and obviously, you may want to comment on the blog itself. So, at the bottom, we provide a simple way to hit the real website, as shown in the following screenshot:

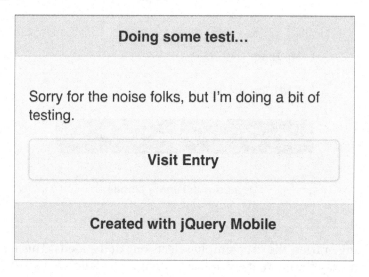

Now that you've seen the application, let's build it. Once again, we're going to use PhoneGap Build to create the final result, but this application will actually run as is on a regular website as well. We will discuss exactly why in a bit.

Creating the RSS reader application

Our application begins with the first page, index.html. This page will load in jQuery and jQuery Mobile as well. Its core mission is to list your current feeds, but it has to recognize when the user has no feeds at all and provide a bit of text encouraging them to add their first feed:

```
Code 13-1: index.html
<!DOCTYPE html>
<html>
<head>
<title>RSS Reader App</title>
<meta name="viewport" content="width=device-width, initial-scale=1">
<link rel="stylesheet"
    href="jquery.mobile/jquery.mobile-1.4.5.min.css" />
<script src="jquery.mobile/jquery-2.1.3.min.js"></script>
<script src="jquery.mobile/jquery.mobile-1.4.5.min.js"></script>
```

```
<script src="main.js"></script>
</head>

<body>

<div data-role="page" id="intropage">

    <div data-role="header">
        <h1>RSS Reader Application</h1>
    </div>

    <div role="main" class="ui-content" id="introContent">
        <p id="introContentNoFeeds" style="display:none">
                Welcome to the RSS Reader Application.
                You do not currently have any RSS Feeds.
                Please use the "Add Feed" button below to begin.
        </p>
        <ul id="feedList" data-role="listview"
        data-inset="true" data-split-icon="delete"></ul>

        <a href="addfeed.html"
        data-role="button" data-theme="b">Add Feed</a>
    </div>

    <div data-role="footer">
        <h4>Created with jQuery Mobile</h4>
    </div>

</div>

<script>
$(document).on("pagecreate", "#intropage", function(e) {
    init();
});
</script>


</body>
</html>
```

As mentioned in the code earlier, we need to load up our jQuery and jQuery Mobile templates first. You can see that in the beginning of the preceding code. Most of the rest of the page is boilerplate HTML you've seen in the previous chapter, so let's call out a few specifics.

First make note of the introductory paragraph. Notice the CSS to hide the text? The assumption here is that — most of the time — the user won't need this text, as they will have feeds. Our code then is going to handle showing it when necessary.

Following that paragraph is an empty list that will display our feeds. Right below this is the button that will be used for adding new feeds.

Finally, we've got a bit of script at the end. This creates an event listener for the jQuery Mobile page event, `pagecreate`, that we tie into to then start up our application tasks.

All of our code (our custom code that is) will be stored in `main.js`. This file is a bit big, so we'll simply show parts of it that relate to each section. Please keep that in mind as we go through the chapter. The entire file can be found with the rest of the book's sample code:

```
Code 13-2: Portion of main.js
function init() {
//handle getting and displaying the intro or feeds
  $(document).on("pageshow", "#intropage", function(e) {
    displayFeeds();
  });
```

Our first snippet from `main.js` comes from the `init` function. Remember, this is run on `pagecreate` for the home page. It's run before the page shows up. This makes it a good place to go ahead and register a function for when the page is displayed. We've taken most of that logic out into its own function, so let's take a look at this next.

The displayFeeds function

The `displayFeeds` function handles retrieving our feeds and displaying them. The logic is simple. If there are no feeds, then we need to display the introductory text. Otherwise, we need to simply render out each feed:

```
Code 13-3: displayFeeds from main.js
function displayFeeds() {
  var feeds = getFeeds();
  if(feeds.length == 0) {
    //in case we had one form before...
    $("#feedList").html("");
    $("#introContentNoFeeds").show();
  } else {
    $("#introContentNoFeeds").hide();
    var s = "";
    for(var i=0; i<feeds.length; i++) {
```

```
      s+= "<li><a href='feed.html?id="+i+"' data-
         feed='"+i+"'>"+feeds[i].name+"</a> <a href=''
         class='deleteFeed'
         data-feedid='"+i+"'>Delete</a></li>";
  }
  $("#feedList").html(s);
    $("#feedList").listview("refresh");
  }
}
```

Notice that we also cleaned out the list. It's possible that a user had feeds and deleted them. By resetting the list to an empty string, we ensure that we don't leave anything behind. If there are feeds, we create the list dynamically, ensuring we call the `listview("refresh")` API at the end to ask jQuery Mobile to enhance the list.

Storing our feeds

So, where do the feeds come from? How do we store them? While we are using PhoneGap and could make use of the embedded SQLite database implementation, we can use something simpler: `localStorage`. This is an HTML5 feature that allows you to store key or value pairs on the client. While you can't store complex data, you can use JSON serialization to encode complex data before it's stored. This makes the storage of data extremely simple.

 Do keep in mind though that `localStorage` involves file storage.

Your application needs to read from a file whenever a change is made to the data. Since we are talking about a simple list of feeds, though, this data should be relatively small:

```
Code 13-3: getFeeds, addFeed, and removeFeed
function getFeeds() {
  if(localStorage["feeds"]) {
    return JSON.parse(localStorage["feeds"]);
  } else return [];
}
function addFeed(name,url) {
  var feeds = getFeeds();
  feeds.push({name:name,url:url});
  localStorage["feeds"] = JSON.stringify(feeds);
}
```

```
function removeFeed(id) {
  var feeds = getFeeds();
  feeds.splice(id, 1);
  localStorage["feeds"] = JSON.stringify(feeds);
  displayFeeds();
}
```

The previous three functions represent the entire wrapper to our storage system. Let's discuss about them in brief:

- `getFeeds`: This function simply checks `localStorage` for the value, and if it exists, it handles converting the JSON data into a native JavaScript object using the `parse` function

- `addFeed`: This function takes a feed name and URL, creates a simple object out of it, and stores the JSON version

- `removeFeed`: This function simply handles finding the right item in the array, removing it, and storing it back to `localStorage`

Storage is done using the `stringify` function. As you can imagine, it takes data and turns it into a string.

Adding an RSS feed

So far, so good. Now let's look at the logic necessary to add a feed. If you remember, the link we used to add a feed went to `addfeed.html`. Let's take a look at it:

```
Code 13-4: addfeed.html
<div data-role="page" id="addfeedpage" data-add-back-btn="true">
  <div data-role="header">
    <h1>Add Feed</h1>
  </div>
  <div data-role="content">
    <form id="addFeedForm">
    <div data-role="fieldcontain">
       <label for="feedname">Feed Name:</label>
       <input type="text" id="feedname" value=""  />
    </div>
    <div data-role="fieldcontain">
      <label for="feedurl">Feed URL:</label>
      <input type="text" id="feedurl" value=""  />
    </div>
    <input type="submit" value="Add Feed" data-theme="b">
  </div>
```

```
<div data-role="footer">
  <h4>Created with jQuery Mobile</h4>
</div>
</div>
```

There isn't much to this page outside of the form. Note that our form has no action. We aren't using a server here. Instead, our code is going to handle picking up the form submission and doing something with it. Also, note that we've not done something we recommended earlier—putting the jQuery and jQuery Mobile includes on top. Those includes are necessary in desktop applications because it's possible the user may bookmark a page outside of your application's home page. Since the eventual target for this code is a PhoneGap application, we don't have to worry about this. This makes our HTML files a bit smaller. Now, let's return to `main.js` and look at the code that handles this logic.

The following code is a snippet from the `init` method of `main.js`. It handles the button click on the form:

```
Code 13-5: Add Feed event registration logic
//Listen for the addFeedPage so we can support adding feeds
$(document).on("pageshow", "#addfeedpage", function(e) {
  $("#addFeedForm").submit(function(e) {
    handleAddFeed();
    return false;
  });
});
```

Now we can take a look at `handleAddFeed`. I've abstracted this code just to make things simpler:

```
Code 13-6: handleAddFeed
function handleAddFeed() {
  var feedname = $.trim($("#feedname").val());
  var feedurl = $.trim($("#feedurl").val());
  //basic error handling
  var errors = "";
  if(feedname == "") errors += "Feed name is required.\n";
  if(feedurl == "") errors += "Feed url is required.\n";
  if(errors != "") {
    //Create a PhoneGap notification for the error
    navigator.notification.alert(errors, function() {});
  } else {
    addFeed(feedname, feedurl);
    $.mobile.changePage("index.html");
  }
}
```

For the most part, the logic here should be simple to understand. We get the feed name and URL values, ensure they aren't blank, and optionally alert any error. If an error didn't occur, then we run the `addFeed` method described earlier. Notice that we make use of the `changePage` API to redirect the user to the home page.

I'll call out one particular bit of code here, the line that handles displaying the error:

```
navigator.notification.alert(errors, function() {});
```

This line comes from the PhoneGap/Cordova plugin for notifications (`https://www.npmjs.com/package/cordova-plugin-dialogs`). It creates a mobile-specific alert notification for your device. You can think of it as a fancier JavaScript `alert()` call. The second argument is a callback function for the alert window dismissal. Because we don't need to do anything in this situation, we provide an empty callback that does nothing.

Viewing a feed

Moving on, what happens when a user clicks to view a feed? This is probably the most complex aspect of the application. We begin with the HTML template, which is rather simple because most of the work is going to be done in JavaScript:

```
Code 13-7: feed.html
<div data-role="page" id="feedpage" data-add-back-btn="true">
  <div data-role="header">
    <h1></h1>
  </div>
  <div data-role="content" id="feedcontents">
  </div>
  <div data-role="footer">
    <h4>Created with jQuery Mobile</h4>
  </div>
</div>
```

This page basically acts as a shell.

 Note that it has no real content at all, just empty HTML elements waiting to be filled.

Let's return to `main.js` and see how this works:

```
Code 13-8: Feed display handler (part 1)
//Listen for the Feed Page so we can displaying entries
$(document).on("pageshow", "#feedpage", function(e) {
```

```
//get the feed id based on query string
var query = $(this).data("url").split("=")[1];
//remove ?id=
query = query.replace("?id=","");
//assume it's a valid ID, since this is a mobile app folks won't
  be messing with the urls, but keep
//in mind normally this would be a concern
var feeds = getFeeds();
var thisFeed = feeds[query];
$("h1",this).text(thisFeed.name);
if(!feedCache[thisFeed.url]) {
    $("#feedcontents").html("<p>Fetching data...</p>");
    //now use Google Feeds API
    $.get("https://ajax.googleapis.com/ajax/services/feed/
        load?v=1.0&num=10&q="+encodeURI(thisFeed.url)+"&callback=?", {},
    function(res,code) {
    //see if the response was good...
    if(res.responseStatus == 200) {
        feedCache[thisFeed.url] = res.responseData.feed.entries;
        displayFeed( thisFeed.url);
    } else {
        var error = "<p>Sorry, but this feed could not be
            loaded:</p><p>"+res.responseDetails+"</p>";
        $("#feedcontents").html(error);
    }
    },"json");
} else {
    displayFeed(thisFeed.url);
    }
});
```

This first snippet handles listening for the `pageshow` event on `feed.html`. This
means that it will run every time the file is viewed, which is what we want, since it is
used for every different feed. How does that work? Remember that our list of feeds
included an identifier for the feed itself:

```
for(var i=0; i<feeds.length; i++) {
    s+= "<li><a href='feed.html?id="+i+"' data-
    feed='"+i+"'>"+feeds[i].name+"</a> <a href=''
    class='deleteFeed'
    data-feedid='"+i+"'>Delete</a></li>";
}
```

jQuery Mobile provides us access to the URL via the `data-url` attribute. Since this returns the entire URL and we only care about stuff after the question mark, we can use some string functions to clean it up. The end result is a numeric value query that we can use to fetch the data out of our feed query. In a regular desktop application, it would be pretty simple for a user to mess with the URL parameters. Therefore, we'd do some checking here to ensure that the value requested actually exists. Since this is a single user application on a mobile device, it really isn't necessary to worry about it.

Before we try to fetch the feed, we make use of a simple caching system. The very first line in `main.js` creates an empty object:

```
//used for caching
var feedCache= {};
```

This object will store the results from our feeds so that we don't have to constantly re-fetch them. That's why the following line of code is run before we do any additional network calls:

```
if(!feedCache[thisFeed.url]) {
```

So, how do we actually get the feed? Google has a cool service called the **Feed API** (`https://developers.google.com/feed/`). It lets us use Google to handle fetching in the XML of an RSS feed, and converting it to JSON. JavaScript can work with XML, but JSON is far easier, since it becomes regular, simple JavaScript objects. We've got a bit of error handling, but if everything works well, we will simply cache the result. The final bit is a call to `displayFeed`:

```
Code 13-9: displayFeed
function displayFeed(url) {
  var entries = feedCache[url];
  var s = "<ul data-role='listview' data-inset='true'
    id='entrylist'>";
  for(var i=0; i<entries.length; i++) {
    var entry = entries[i];
    s += "<li><a
      href='entry.html?entry="+i+"&url="+encodeURI(url)+"'>"+
      entry.title+"</a></li>";
  }
  s += "</ul>";
  $("#feedcontents").html(s);
  $("#entrylist").listview();
}
```

All that the previous block of code does is iterate over the result feed. When Google parsed the XML from the feed, it turned into an array of objects we can loop over. While there are a number of properties in the feed we may be interested in for the list we care about the `title` property only. Notice how we build our link. We pass the numeric index and the URL (that we will be using in the next portion). This is then rendered to a simple jQuery Mobile `listview`.

Creating the entry view

Ready for the last part? Let's look at the individual entry display. As before, we'll begin with the template:

```
Code 13-10: entry.html
<div data-role="page" id="entrypage" data-add-back-btn="true">
  <div data-role="header">
    <h1></h1>
  </div>
  <div data-role="content">
    <div id="entrycontents"></div>
    <a href="" id="entrylink" data-role="button">Visit Entry</a>
  </div>
  <div data-role="footer">
    <h4>Created with jQuery Mobile</h4>
  </div>
</div>
```

Similar to `feed.html` before it, `entry.html` is an empty shell. Note that the header, the content, and the link are empty. All of these will be replaced with real code. Let's head back to `main.js` and look at the code that handles this page:

```
Code 13-11: Entry page event handler
$(document).on("pageshow", "#entrypage", function(e) {
    //get the entry id and url based on query string
    var query = $(this).data("url").split("?")[1];
    //remove ?
    query = query.replace("?","");
    //split by &
    var parts = query.split("&");
    var entryid = parts[0].split("=")[1];
    var url = parts[1].split("=")[1];
    var entry = feedCache[url][entryid];
    $("h1",this).text(entry.title);
    $("#entrycontents",this).html(entry.content);
    $("#entrylink",this).attr("href",entry.link);
});
```

So, what's going on here? Remember that we passed an index value (which entry was clicked, the first or the second?) and the URL of the feed. We parse out these values from the URL. Once we know the URL of the feed, we can use our cache to get the specific entry. Once we have this, it's a simple matter to update the header, contents, and link. And that's it!

Going further

You can take the code from this application and upload it to the PhoneGap Build service now to try it out on your own device. But what else could we have done? Here's a short list of things to consider:

- PhoneGap/Cordova provides a connection plugin API (`https://www.npmjs.com/package/cordova-plugin-network-information`) that returns information about the device's connection status. You could add support for this to prevent the user from trying to read a feed when the device isn't online.

- While we store the user's feeds in `localStorage`, the cached data from reading the RSS entry is stored temporarily. You could also store this data and use it when the user is offline.

- PhoneGap/Cordova has an excellent plugin API, and a great variety of plugins is already available (`http://plugins.cordova.io/`). One of these plugins allows for easier sending of SMS messages. You could add an option to send an entry title and link to a friend via SMS.

Hopefully, you get the idea. This is only one example of the power of jQuery Mobile and PhoneGap.

Summary

In this chapter, we took what you had learned about PhoneGap from the previous chapter and created a full, if rather simple, mobile application making use of jQuery Mobile for designing and interactivity.

Index

jQuery UI
URL 119

L

linear gradients 188
list dividers
autodividers 48, 49
list features
inset lists, creating 46
list dividers, creating 47, 48
lists, creating with count bubbles 50, 51
split button lists, creating 54, 55
thumbnails and icons, using 51-53
working with 46
lists
about 41
creating 41-45

M

mini fields
working with 89
mobile application
defining 123
designing 124
HTML, writing 127-130
requirements, listing 124, 125
URL 123
multiple files
working with 18-21
multiple pages
adding, to one file 14-17

N

namespace 132
navigation bar footers
persisting, across multiple pages 38-40
navigation bars
working with 36-38
note
.on() method, using 142
deleting 146
viewing 141
note data
storing 133

Notekeeper
theme, creating for 202-204
Notekeeper app
custom theme, adding 206, 207
updating 206
Notekeeper data
localStorage, using 133, 134
storing 133

P

page container 158
page events
$(document).ready, defining 177
categories 174, 175
handling 174-177
real example, creating 178-180
panels
working with 113-116
PhoneGap
APIs, defining 210
URL 209
PhoneGap Build
about 212
URL 212
PhoneGap documentation
URL 211
physical events
working with 167-173
popups
using 105-108

R

radial gradients 188
Really Simple Syndication (RSS) 223
requirements, mobile application
Add Note wireframe, designing 126
Display Notes wireframe 126
listing 124, 125
View Note/Delete button wireframe 127
wireframes, building 125
responsive grids
creating 97, 98
responsive tables
defining 109-113

RSS reader
defining 223-226
RSS reader application
creating 226-228
displayFeeds function 228, 229
entry view, creating 235
feeds, storing 229, 230
feed, viewing 232-234
RSS feed, adding 230-232

S

select menus, jQuery Mobile
custom select fields 81, 82
defining 75-81
self-executing function 131
serialization 133
split button list 54
Static Maps
about 62
URL 62

T

tabs
working with 119-121
text shadows 185

ThemeRoller
about 195
URL 183
using 196, 197
ThemeRoller, for jQuery Mobile
URL 195
toolbars 25

V

virtual events 168

X

XML HTTP Request (XHR) 20

Z

ZIP file option
URL 4

CPSIA information can be obtained
at www.ICGtesting.com
Printed in the USA
LVOW04s0211040118
561612LV00007B/70/P